MAGGIE'S STORY:

TEACHINGS OF A CHEROKEE HEALER

BY

PAMELA DAWES TAMBORNINO

Mammoth Publications

Lawrence, Kansas

ISBN 978-0-9845912-1-3

Published by Mammoth Publications, Lawrence, Kansas

Distributed by Mammoth Publications
1916 Stratford Rd., Lawrence, KS 66044

mammothpubs@hotmail.com
www.mammothpublications.com

Cover painting by Thomas Pecore Weso
Author photograph by Maggie Kruger

The author makes grateful acknowledgement to the following
publications where some of these stories first appeared:
   Yellow Medicine Review, edited by Ralph Salisbury, "Noodling"
   Tribal College Journal, "My Cherokee Grandmother"

*For my family—
who love and continue to teach me
then and now.*

CONTENTS

MY CHEROKEE GRANDMOTHER
TSA LA GI E LI SI

My first memories of my grandmother are of her jet black hair, her huge smile, and her dark eyes. She was full of contradictions: she laughed a lot; worked hard; played hard; had definite ideas of what a family was to be like; and she had an opinion that was always right. She also had a temper and was not afraid to use it when wronged. Everyone that knew her ran when she growled low and soft in her throat and called them "Heifer" in her clear bell voice. This was a strong signal that things were going to start flying around the room. My father always used to say she never knew she was so small and vulnerable looking—she felt and acted like the strong woman she was. She was protective of me, the first grandchild and first granddaughter, and taught me the healing ways and started me down the road of traditional learning and ways of the Cherokee people. I remember the first time that my grandmother took me hunting for herbs and medicines in the woods. She was short, four feet two inches, but she would always say four and a half feet tall when asked—and one hundred pounds of pure love. She was Cherokee and was a healer of our tribe, and everyone called her Maggie. I was a thin little girl of six—dragging a basket, spade and woven bag following behind her.

As we walked in the woods she always told me stories while teaching me the healing ways. One day she would say, "We are from the Wolf Clan, a strong clan to be proud of—do not disrespect our family name." Then she would say, "Dig here. That root is good for stopping bleeding in childbirth," and I would start digging in the hard red clay of Pawhuska, Oklahoma, for that root. I learned much of our language from my grandmother and her mother; I am now relearning the language that I have forgotten since she died. I also learned how to mix herbs and barks and plants to bring down fevers (*ka-na-si-ta*, dogwood); help upset stomachs (*sa-li, gu gu ga nu lv, da-ga si a la s de na*—peppermint, tickweed, and terrapin's foot); arthritis (*u did le hv s'gi i lv s'gi,* feverfew); liver ailments (*go s'du i-tlv- gv*, ash tree); and a variety of other ailments. Her kitchen was forever littered with hanging plants and bags of various dried barks and plants. It smelled spicy, woodsy, and wonderful. Often, as she boiled a remedy, I would be asked to bring this plant or that plant to her, and she would indicate how the remedy should be applied and how it worked.

She also made sure that each year I was dosed with the appropriate preventative medicines—some of which she had to chase me down to pour in my mouth. She would say, "This one is for the purification of the liver. This one strengthens the blood." Not all medicines, I learned, smelled and tasted good even if they were good for the body.

She also taught me many traditional stories of the Cherokee, among them: the trickster stories, the little people stories, and the creation story. I remember raptly sitting at her feet listening to her strong voice flow over me with the images of the characters of coyote, the rabbit, the turtle and grandmother spider dancing in my head. The stories still stir in my mind as the words turn to real images, and I can feel again the soft summer's wind in my hair and smell the barks and plants on her hands as she gestured. It was a magical time that passed too swiftly, as years now pass swiftly in my old age.

I can still see her home—an old homestead, painted all white that she stood in line to bid on for twelve hours when she was young and married with four children. In my mind's eye I see the large leafy trees, the huge ant hill at the top of the gravel driveway, and the front porch that my father made, and also the hanging swing he made in high school. The swing still hangs there today. Many hours were spent on that porch with family until late into the night, talking and remembering. Some of my fondest memories were made in this house—the first time I went to a fish fry at midnight, the first time I fished for fourteen hours with family and enjoyed it, the first time I ran a combine and picked wheat, the first time I killed a snake (even if it was little), the first time I really learned to listen, and of course, first and foremost: love of family comes first.

A REAL BAPTIST LADY
WHO KNEW THE FOUR DIRECTIONS
NV GI WI DU YU GU DV

Grandma was brought up to be a real Baptist lady, but she also knew about Native religion. I came to find out that she claimed she was Baptist (on government forms and in front of formal White company) but she told friends she practiced the Native religion her mom taught her. What I got was the lesson of what a "real proper lady" should be in this world, but also I can worship in the Cherokee way. Mostly, the commonality of all religions stuck with me.

My first lesson on the Four Directions came at an early age while gathering plants for healing. Grandma would point at the directions and explain: East was linked with the color red, the power of the rising sun; North was linked with the color white, for strength; West was black and the direction of sundown; and, South was yellow for comfort. These colors made up the medicine wheel and the circle of life, rebirth and unity of the Cherokee tribe. This was a lot to take in at such an early age, and she repeated the wheel many times and expanded on its meaning as I grew.

By the time I was a teenager I also knew that Winter (*go-la*) was the Cherokee connection to the direction of north, which meant cold (*u-yv-tlv*); that Spring (*gi-la-go-ge*) and East (*ka-lv-gv*) were linked to new life; that Summer (*go-ga*) was linked to the word warm (*u-ga-no-wa*) and meant peace; and Autumn (*u-la-go-hv-s'di*) was west (*wu-de-li-gv*) and stood for the cycle of life.

She explained to me that all life was a circle. A person is conceived, is born, grows, and cycles through the seasons over and over until the transition of death to another place—a good place. Life never truly ends; it continues in a circle. She said that

Cherokee Nation is like this circle: no matter what befalls the Nation, the circle will continue as the Creator intended.

So it came to be that I viewed each season with new eyes. As spring came, I saw that Mother Earth renewed everything, and a rebirth took place among her inhabitants. The plants grew, flowers bloomed, seeds dropped, and the Earth was alive. And so it was with each season, not just a time of frost, snow, cold and warmth, but a part of the cycle that my life was running. In my own life it was meant for me to be born, grow, repeat the cycles, mature, grow old and transition into death—all in the Creator's time.

We spent many hours discussing the Bible and the Four Directions and Medicine Wheel. She did not have much schooling, as her parents pulled her from school in the eighth grade to work on their farm, but her wisdom was beyond that of almost anyone I have ever met.

My knowledge expanded through the years, as children's building blocks stacked upon each other, and I was taught the ceremonies of our tribe: of birth, the use of the spirit fire, the pureness of tobacco, reverence for life, and the bonding of the members of the tribe through hardship and happiness.

I remember crying as my great-great-grandmother told of the Trail of Tears, the story that her mother had told her, and of the many along the way that had starved or frozen. At first I could not believe the hardships and broken promises our Nation had faced, along with broken treaties and boarding schools. Yet the ring of truth was heavy in my great-great- grandmother's solemn words. I learned that wisdom comes with a price.

In Lawrence, Kansas, at the university where I work, there is a full earthworks medicine wheel with the four direction marked by granite pillars. Many times, I travel to that wheel and give praise for my blessings and ask help in times of trouble. How do I reconcile this with the practice of Christianity that I also believe in? It is not hard. Each religion shares so many things in common.

They share aims of living the way I want others to treat me; the
love of Mother Earth; the belief in the great Creator; the oneness
of all things, and their place in the circle of life. All of this flows in
my beliefs smoothly and easily. One form of worship honors my
mother and her ancestors, and the other honors my father and his
ancestors. Both honor life and the spirit and gifts received through
the circle of my life.

CHEROKEE NIGHTS

TSA LA GI SV NO I

My grandmother was a special woman, not just because she was a
healer, but because she knew the stories and ways of the Nation.
Many nights we would lie on a blanket outside and look at the
stars. These were special times. She would point at the big dipper
and talk about the story behind it, and then in the same breath
would talk about how stars began in the sky—the old stories of
the elders.

We always did these watchings after dishes were done, and if
the sky was completely clear. We did it in the summer when the
soft winds ruffled our hair and our bare feet met the grass. These
were the times that were for her and me alone. Time stood still
when we did this—sometimes it was a few hours, and a couple of
times it was until dawn. All of the time we spent learning about
the old ways and enjoying each other's company. This was when I
learned the Cherokee Creation Story, and how the Sky People
lived.

One night she told me a special story about Rabbit, and it
stuck with me completely on the first telling. This is what she
said:

> Rabbit was a good food for the wolves, and Rabbit had to
> be careful when out and about at night, so that wolves did
> not get him. Well, one night Rabbit ran into many wolves
> that were very hungry. Rabbit looked around and started to
> sing:

> On the edge of the field I dance about —
> *Ha nia lil! Lil! Ha nia Lil! Lil!*

Rabbit looked at the Wolf nearest to him and said he would dance with him, so the wolves started to dance with Rabbit. Each time Rabbit danced, he got closer and closer to the forest, saying to the wolves, "Dance harder and you will be happy and hungry no more."

So the dance went—on and on as Rabbit danced and the wolves danced with him, until Rabbit was so near the forest he could jump over the wolves. Rabbit jumped over the wolves and hopped as fast as he could to the hollow tree, and in it Rabbit took refuge. The wolves were angry as they knew they had been tricked. One Wolf went right up to the hollow tree and put his head in, trying to get Rabbit, but Rabbit spit in his eye and he had to leave.

This is how Rabbit outsmarted the wolves.

I was impressed with the story, as we were of the Wolf clan, and I knew that wolves were to be avoided and not killed if possible. Another Wolf would seek revenge, and the weapon that killed the Wolf could not be used again unless a medicine man blessed it.

Many nights I now lie awake looking out of the window across the country, looking at the sky and hearing the wind ring the wind chimes in the big tree out back. It is then I feel that Grandma is by my side again, telling me her stories and giving me the dreams that cause me to cherish her wisdom and worth. How lucky I was to have her.

MY FIRST DELIVERY—A NEW LIFE
A TSE V KE NI TO HV

Many times Grandma was called upon by neighbors to help with the birthing of animals, since most could not afford a veterinarian. One night she got a message to come to a neighbor's farm because his cow was having trouble. She buzzed around gathering this and that, including a large cast iron boiling pot, and off we went to the neighbors. This was about 1:00 a.m., and it was blasted cold out—it was in January and the temperature had dipped below zero the day before.

We reached the neighbor's house within fifteen minutes and got to the barn to see him trying to pull a calf out of the cow by the hind legs—it was a breech birth. This calf meant a lot to this family, who had very little.

Soon Grandma was barking orders to the man's wife to get water boiling, into which she put blue cohosh (*ga-le-gi*) and willow bark. As this boiled, she saw that the calf was not moving much, so she took hold of one leg, the owner took hold of the other leg, and I held the cow's head. Then everybody pulled: they pulled back, and I pulled forward. In a few minutes the calf was out, but still not moving.

Grandma took a warm cloth and starting cleaning out its nose and mouth and rubbing it all over. She shook it and scratched at its hide softly, and yelled at it to "Get the hell up and quit messing around." In the meantime she asked me to pour some of the boiling mixture down the cow's throat to help with bleeding and pain. I did this after letting it cool off and putting it in an empty Pepsi bottle (they were still glass then).

In a few minutes we despaired that the calf could be saved, but sure enough, Grandma's shaking and stroking worked. The calf bleated and starting moving. The cow turned her head, and she moved to it and started licking it. It was then that Grandma announced it would be okay. She had the owner hold the calf up to nurse, she said that this would help stop the cow's bleeding. I could not see how this would work—but it did.

After much sweating, pulling, yanking, and ladling the medicine down the cow's throat, we had a new life. The owner was so thankful, he and his wife gave us two jars of peaches that his wife had canned. This was often how she was paid—she never asked for any payment. She said what she did was a gift to be shared, not sold.

Walking back home, I took note that we were a mess. Grandma's arms and hands were covered with mud, blood, and straw. They hung limply at her sides. I looked like a clone of her—pooped. We both cleaned up at home, and as I went to bed, she came and said that I had helped save my first life. I felt good knowing that I had some little part in helping out a mother and baby have a happy ending.

A NIGHT IN THE RAIN
A GA S'GA

One night there was a knock at the door in the early morning
hours. It was a small child asking that Grandma come, as her
mother was very ill. I was there at the time, and there was always
a large bag packed with packets of herbs, plants and roots, as well
as the materials that would be needed for preparation and
application, ready by the door. We grabbed the bag and arrived at
house in one of the poorest parts of Pawhuska. Inside, the child
showed us a woman in her early thirties who was very pale,
feverish, and shivering.

Grandma assessed the situation by feeling the woman's head,
looking at her fingernails and eyes, listening to her lungs, and
asking the child a few questions. The child said that her mother
had some heart trouble and took a pill to get rid of water, and that
she had been unable to breathe well.

Grandma went to her bag and pulled out blue flag, devil's bit,
white snakeroot and ginseng. These she crushed up in a bowl and
boiled in a pot on the stove. These are good diuretics when put in
tea or coffee and also help with breathing, as Grandma thought
the sounds of her lungs were labored. Pneumonia sounds like a
rattle or cracking when a person breathes a deep breath, and this
woman certainly sounded like that in her breathing.

Grandma looked around the kitchen and found a bag of
onions, which she put me to chopping into pieces. While I did
that, she brewed dogwood, valerian, willow bark and black
cohosh to help with the pain and fever that the woman was
running. As soon as this was mixed, it too was added to the tea
that the woman sipped.

In the bag Grandma always kept clean linen strips, and she
pulled these out and spread them on the table. She asked me to fry
the pieces of onion in the black skillet on the stove until the pieces

were very hot, and to let her know when I was ready. It took about fifteen minutes, and many of the pieces were hot and steamy. These pieces she placed on the linen and folded the linen over onto itself to form a kind of pouch. She made about six of these pouches and placed them on the woman's chest.

The night went on, with me frying onions and Grandma replacing onion packets on the woman's chest. About five hours went by, and the woman started to cough a very deep cough. I looked at Grandma in alarm, but she was smiling. She told me to bring a bucket from outside, and she reached behind the woman and pushed her into sitting position. The coughing got deeper and deeper. She placed the bucket in front of the woman. In a very short time, the woman was coughing up a thick fluid that was dark and had a slightly acid smell. Grandma explained that this was what was in her lungs, and that this had to be removed before the lungs would heal.

After about twenty minutes of coughing, the process started again with frying onions, making packets and placing them on the woman's chest—again she would start coughing. This went on throughout the night until at last, the woman stopped coughing up phlegm and her breathing started sounding better.

Grandma made a broth for the woman, and she was able to drink this. To increase her appetite, she crushed bilberry and nettle, which she had the woman sip a little at a time. Every so often, she would give her the pain medication to make her drowsy and also to allow her to relax.

Morning came, and the child had been long asleep. Grandma checked the woman and found that the fever had broken, and the woman was breathing normally. About that time her husband came home from work. Grandma left a bottle of pain tonic for him to give her a teaspoon at a time in tea or coffee.

We went home about nine hours later, and I asked if the woman would continue to get better. My grandma told me that she thought so, if they could get her to eat and sleep more during the coming days.

Checking in the next day, we found the woman was sitting up in bed and holding a cup of water. She smiled as she saw us. She told us she and her husband had no insurance, and not being Native, they could not go to the Indian Clinic for medications. She and her husband thanked us over and over for our help, and it was good to see that such a sick person could really benefit from the cures that so long had been used by the Cherokee.

That was the last time I saw that family, as her husband was moved to another road job and his family followed, but I heard that the woman looked healthy and walked with her child as they boarded the bus. It was a good feeling to be able to help Grandma and know we had made a difference.

Now I understood why Grandma did not like the smell of cooking onions—I agreed and still do not to this day.

A BABY BORN
U S'DI I U DE NV

Grandma always said that babies were born at very inconvenient times. By inconvenient she meant that they were born during bad weather (hailing, lightening, strong rain, tornado warnings); in the middle of the night when you were sleeping the best; when she already had plans set up with family; or any time that was not the best time. One summer I saw what she meant.

It was about two o'clock in the morning, and my whole family was in the "hole" under the front porch that Grandma had dug out and cemented, for tornados. She was once in a tornado that left her and her youngest child holding onto the bathroom sink pipes, and everything else was completely gone when she opened her eyes. It was a miracle that she came out without a scratch. It was her belief that she should not push her luck, and it only had to lightening once, and everybody went into the "hole." And it was exactly that, a hole, with room for about seven people, standing up, with an old bed springs down there without a mattress. I remember that the springs always had spiders on them.

Of course, it was bring your own light, or the dark was what you got. That morning we had just gotten out of the hole, after an hour, when Grandma deemed it was semi-safe. It was just raining, and the telephone was ringing. She answered it, said a few mumbled things, and said she would come.

A woman was giving birth, and Grandma's services were needed. She was first and foremost a person that helped people, so donning her rain gear, and taking a bag of medicines, out she went into the storm looking for a home in the Lynn section of Pawhuska. I went with her.

It took a while to find the house, but finally we did and pulled up in front. After knocking on the door, it was opened by a young man who looked frantic and was blurting that he did not know what to do, and they did not have insurance Grandma moved him aside, literally with her arm, and started looking for the mother to be.

We found her sitting on the toilet. She said she could not stop "peeing." Grandma got her off the toilet, telling her that her water had broken, and she did not want to deliver the baby into the pottie did she? The baby was so low and ready to be born, that we only got her on the bathroom floor. She could not even walk.

Grandma had the husband boil water—I asked her why because she never used it before. She said to keep him busy. That seemed to make sense, as he was sure a twit when it came to emergencies.

Grandma pulled out of her bag clean toweling, sterilized scissors, clean shoe strings, and a new baby blanket. She also had a rubber bulb that, when squeezed, sucked out mucus from the baby's mouth and nose. She also had cleanser she used to wash her hands and forearms. She said I could help with this delivery, and I also washed using the cleanser. She sent me back three times, saying I had to be "very clean."

The labor commenced and the woman pushed and pushed. All the while, the husband boiled water and ran back and forth from the room. Grandma said it was a straight forward delivery; she could see the baby's head and had felt around the neck to make sure the cord was not around it.

On and on it went. Eight hours passed, and the head of the baby was born. Grandma said push hard, and the shoulders slipped out, and the rest of the little one followed with ease. Grandma checked the baby, suctioned its mouth and nose, and rubbed it vigorously all over to get it stimulated and crying. It let out a hell of a wail, and all had smiles on their faces. She tied the cord with the shoes strings and cut between the strings. Grandma looked at the mother and said, "It is a little boy, and all of his fingers and toes are there!" She got the little one clean and wrapped him like a mummy in the clean blanket. Then she gave the little one to his mother, who alternately cried and laughed with joy.

Grandma noticed that there was a little more bleeding than usual and asked the husband to come in and help us. He ran into the room, with a pan of boiling water, which she told him to put down and sit next to his wife on the floor. Now here is the weird part. She asked him to play with his wife's breasts to help stop the bleeding. That was a first for me. I could not believe she was asking him to do that. I thought perhaps it was a new ploy to keep him sane and functional?

Anyway, with a little encouragement, he started massaging his wife's breasts. The new mother hardly knew he was doing anything, but he looked as embarrassed as anyone could get. Grandma looked at him and said, "Keep at it, young man. Surely this is not the first time you have done this, and you are helping us stop the bleeding." If possible the guy turned redder, but he kept at the massaging. Sure enough, about ten minutes later, the bleeding slowed and then stopped.

Grandma delivered the afterbirth, cleaned up the new mother, got her into bed with the new baby, and made sure that the baby knew how to nurse before she left. Believe it not, not all new mothers have the knack the first time in knowing how to get the baby to nurse.

All in all, it was about ten hours worth of coaching the mother, dosing her with passionflower and valerian for her pain and to help her relax, and getting things in order. As we were leaving, the husband frantically asked what to do with the boiling water and Grandma said," Throw it out. It was just to help keep you occupied while your wife and I got the work done." The husband paled, and said that he was never going to have another baby again, and Grandma said, "You still have one, so you can't have another!" With that parting shot, she turned and went back home. I later learned that they had named the baby Maggie, and I could tell that Grandma looked a little smug and said, "That husband did have some sense after all."

COMMODITIES

One of the things that Grandma really hated was getting commodities. Once a month a person would show up at the door and give her a box full of food from the government. Of course, this was distributed by the tribe, and she knew it, but still she did not want it. I found out there was a reason. In the box would often be: a gallon can of peanut butter, flour, salt, sugar, dried beans, canned meat (very generic), a huge block of American cheese (or something similar to cheese), a large brick of lard, and various vegetables with labels that had pictures of the vegetable on them—in case the person could not read "green beans."

When I was at Grandma's house, she wanted me to eat all of this food, as she had no use for it. This was not her way of cooking, and she could not open most of it. For instance, the gallon can of peanut butter, when opened, had about an inch-and-a-half of oil on top, so it had to be stirred to be eaten. She was in her eighties, and she could not stir the sticky mass. Also, it took a screw driver to open the lid (it was just like paint can). Next, the large brick of lard that always accompanied the food had to be sliced to be used and took quite a bit of strength to cut. That went for the cheese, as well.

Since she could read but not spell well, she hated the pictures on the cans indicating that she had to have drawings to know what was in the can. The outcome of this was often she had stacks and stacks of commodities piled on her back porch where the washer and dryer were. Often, I had to dig out the commodities to wash and dry clothes.

She was a proud woman who canned her own fruits and vegetables, made her own bread, and often used traditional plants that grew everywhere for food—such as pokeweed and wild onions. She used to send the commodities home with anyone of her children that would use them, or they sat on the porch until they expired or she got mad and tossed them over the "hill"—a steep hillside that ran by her house and sloped toward Bird Creek. Besides, she said, she was not going to eat anything that came out of a paint can—"It couldn't be healthy." I didn't know about that, but I really did not like wild onions with eggs on them either. But sometimes I wished for the peanut butter.

LEARNING TO WALK SOFTLY
E LA DI E DA S'DI WA NI GE I

There were some summers when money was tight and
commodities did not substitute for meat on the table. It was
during these times Grandma told me I needed to learn how to
hunt with grandpa to get some meat. There were two big things I
had against this mandate: 1) I was scared to death of guns and 2) I
hated the idea of killing any animal. I could not step on a
cockroach, for heaven's sake. But this summer, I could not find an
excuse that worked, so off Grandpa and I went into his favorite
part of the woods to look for rabbits, squirrels, or deer.

His idea of a good gun for this was a 22 rifle that fired about
ten shots without reloading. It was old, as it had been his father's
gun, but he said, "She will get the job done." I always wonder why
men called their guns "she," and I still have not found the answer.

As we went through the woods, grandpa said to walk softly,
don't talk, and do as he did. I thought I could do that, so we
started through some trees, no problem. Then we started through
thick bush, and I became a little nosier, and finally we got to fallen
logs with moss on them, branches everywhere and very uneven
ground. I scampered after him as quickly as I could, but his legs
were twice as long as mine, and I was busy watching for things
that could kill me—like a bear, snake or some other critter I had
never seen. It is spooky in the woods, and I did not have a gun.

Finally, I fell completely over and down a small hill, and
grandpa tromped over and peered down at me and said, "Make
enough noise for this trip?" I thought this was unfair and said so,
as I was having a really rough time keeping up. He said, "If you
want to eat, you have to learn quickly, as bullets cost money, and
there are only so many to go around." I was thinking, fine, why
was I here, if bullets were scarce: I sure did not need to be
shooting them, since I had never even held a gun. I bet I could fit

the cliché "Could not hit the broad side of a barn" with no problem.

I soon found out why I was along. We came across tracks of a deer, and Grandpa said it was headed north toward the stream, and we could walk downwind and get it there. We did more of the "softly walking" through the woods thing, and he stopped so fast, my head hit his butt. He gave me a quick glare, but quickly pointed over to the stream a few yards beyond us.

There was a beautiful deer drinking gracefully. It was hard for me to bear, thinking that he was going to kill such a beautiful animal, but Grandma's words were with me when she explained why animals are in the woods: "Animals are in the woods to help folk feed their families. Don't ever kill for sport, don't kill a female animal with young, and don't take more than you need." I knew we needed this for the family.

Grandpa took careful aim, resting his rifle on an old log, and shot once. There was a loud popping sound, and the deer dropped right where it was standing. We went over, and Grandpa had gotten it in the head. It was dead. He told me it was a young male deer, pointing out the stubs that would have been horns, and he started to dress the deer to take back to the house.

I tried to help him, but at that time, my hands just did not have the strength to help cut up the deer and chop off the parts we would not use. Finally, he had both hind legs, the liver, and heart. He put the liver and heart in a bag, which was mine to carry, along with the hooves, which would be used for stomp dance regalia for friends. He hoisted the two legs over each shoulder.

I don't know how he managed to carry that much weight for a couple of miles; I was having real trouble carrying the twenty pounds or so in the sack. Not even to mention trying to avoid getting dripping blood all over me.

Finally, we made it back to the house, and he started cutting the deer meat into strips to smoke. I gave the heart and liver to

Grandma, who promptly wanted to show me how to cook them. Great, all I needed was to see these cooked, but there was no denying Grandma.

She cut the liver into strips, like strips of bacon, floured them, and placed each strip into a pan with bubbling bacon grease. She said to cook until golden brown, turning once, and then serve while warm. After she had demonstrated the liver, she showed me the heart. I have to admit that the heart thing was bothering me, as I was still seeing those classic stories in my head like Poe's "Telltale Heart." However, Grandma proceeded to put the heart on a cutting board. She cut it like bread, a slice at a time. When she had done this, she washed it well, put it in salt water, and after soaking for a while, washed it off and said it always went well in scrambled eggs or as an addition to any poke salad or ground meat. She froze all but a few pieces, and those she put into the scrambled eggs the next day after chopping them into small pieces. It was funny that I got the flu that next day and could not eat. I swear that woman had radar, or could read minds, because she said, "No problem, there is plenty of heart left." She would cook me some when I felt better. That was when I really started feeling sick.

Eventually, I did taste heart and eggs, as well as fried liver, and I found that I could eat them if I swallowed fast or was quick enough to put it in the napkin in the lap. At least she never caught me doing that. I can't tell you what she would have done, but I am sure that the heifer word would come into play.

The smoked deer was not bad at all. It was kind of like beef jerky.

Anyway, Grandpa thought that my brother was a better hunter, and I should probably stay at home and help Grandma with the garden. I told him this sounded really good, and so it came to be that I was the lousiest hunter in the family. I told Grandma I did not care, because I was going to be a vegetarian. She told me that my mind would "rot from lack of protein." So I compromised. I only ate meat that I had not seen killed, and she kindly fed me meat that I had not seen on the hoof. We agreed on this without a word, and that was one of the things I liked best about Grandma—she could tell a person's comfort level, and let them stay there if she could. God bless her little Cherokee body—no more hiking, no more blood, no more gagging. I just might live to eat another day.

FOOD FROM THE LAND
U LV QUO DV GI

Grandma and I had different opinions about what she thought was good food and what I thought was good food. She made many traditional dishes, and some were really good. The one thing that we could not agree on was frog's legs. Grandma loved her fried frog legs (*ka-nu-na de-ga-la-ya-dv*), and this is what happened when she told me to cook frog legs.

She said her mother's mother had fixed them, and they were "comfort food for the whole family." I always though comfort food was mac and cheese.

When she mentioned frog legs, I had visions of frogs with little blocks of wood in their front legs on a small wheeled wagon, pushing themselves around. Frogs were cute—sort of. Frogging was done in the dusk when it was cool, and the frogs came out to sing. I thought a frog was a frog, but there were only certain frogs that were good enough to eat. The frogs she wanted me to catch were those bull frogs that were bigger than my head.

One night we went out with nets, mesh bags, and gear to get a "mess of frogs" for dinner the next night. The trick was to sneak up on those little devils before they knew anyone was around—because their legs were muscled and they could jump right out of reach in a split second.

I watched Grandma demonstrate how to catch the big ones. She walked softly, barefoot, up the creek bank, paused, moved forward a little more, a little more, and boom, the net went over the poor beast without a blink of an eye. She liked them about three to four pounds each. I did the same as she did—walked barefoot on the creek bed, but instead of the frogs having my full attention, I watched for critters around the watering hole. It took me a good four tries to get close enough to get a frog, and it was a mighty poor specimen at that. I heard a frog singing, but could not see it. I followed the croaking sound, a little forward, a little forward, and bam! I slipped on the bank, face in the mud. But a miracle happened. My net actually caught a frog.

Grandma came over to see my catch and asked why I had mud all over me. I told her I had to jump to get that critter, and she gave me one of those "Ha!" looks and knew I was lying. I showed her my net, and she fished out the frog. The poor thing was barely grown enough to make a big croaking sound. As she held it in her hands, it was making small "ribbit-ribbit" sounds. She concluded that she needed to show me again the size she liked.

I again looked at the big frog, and started out again. Grandma was mirroring her actions on the other side of the creek. I saw her catch another one. I was determined that I was not going to be completely outshone.

This time, I spotted a really big one sitting on a large rock at the creek's edge and started stalking it as quietly as I could. As the mud mashed through my toes, an unpleasant feeling. I imagined what could be in the mud wiggling and alive. I actually got close enough to get the net over the big guy.

Grandma said that it was at least a four-pounder, so he could go in the mesh bag. His skin was a little slimy, and I wondered briefly if the old tales of getting warts from frogs were true. Not to be detoured, I caught about three more before I was pooped out.

Grandma thought we had enough, so we went home. She wanted to clean them before bedtime. I was not looking forward to "cleaning" them, as I knew she was going to kill them.

We reached a large tree stump in the back yard, and Grandma had a small hammer, butcher knife, a large pan, and the water hose going. She fished out a frog and said she would demonstrate how to get the legs cut off so the optimum meat was acquired. She put the frog on the stump, took the hammer and wacked him on the head quickly. She got him the first time, and she said it was the most humane way to kill frogs.

She then got the butcher knife and cleanly cut the back legs off with quick chops. She then skinned the legs and put them under the hose to clean them. These legs went in the big pan. She did two more and said it was time that I learned how to do this.

Well, I did not think I was a wimp. I had cleaned a deer, but frogs are little and somehow to me more fragile looking. With shaking hand, I took a frog from the bag, put him on the stump, and prepared to give him a whack on the head. As the hammer came down, I shut my eyes, so I would not see the creature's death, and hit my left arm a right smart hit—I knew it was broken, because the hand sort of hung limply. Grandma said I was not a good frog cleaner, and we went to the hospital for an x-ray to make sure that my arm was broken. It was, and I got a cast. I was relieved, in a way, it was broken, for no more frog cleaning for me that day.

The one thing that you can count on is that Grandma was unpredictable when it came to what she expected of me, and what she knew I needed to learn. The next day, she said I would be cooking the legs for dinner that night. I thought I could do that one-armed, knowing that I did not kill any of the owners of the legs.

I rolled the legs in mixture of egg and crushed cracker crumbs. Then into a sizzling pan of lard they went.

Grandma got me back on this one. I had just put the first leg in the pan and was turning to put the next one in, and darn if I did not feel something hit me in the back of head. I turned around, and the leg I had put in the pan was now on the floor. It had jumped!

I was young and scared that the frog's spirit was coming back to get me. Saying a prayer, I put the leg back in the pan, with the new rolled leg and sure enough, they both started twitching.

I got a wooden spoon and started to hold them down. I had a time of it as one leg twitched and then the other, and then both at the same time. One-handed, I more than had my hands full. I was not going to call Grandma on this. I was determined to do this on my own.

I decided the best way to do this was to put a lid on the big fryer. So I got all fourteen of the legs rolled and added them at the same time, smashed the lid on the fryer, and sat down at the kitchen table to wait until they had to be turned.

I had been sitting about five minutes, and the lid started to jiggle up and down. I decided that now was the time to call Grandma. She came in and asked if I had cut the nerves in the joints of the legs before I put them in the pan, and I said, "What nerve?" She said she had told me last night that frog legs had nerves in them that caused them to jump when cooked if not cut. I said, "No, guess I did not hear you."

She gave me a look like I was really stupid, and took the lid off of the big cast iron fryer. Well, the only way to describe the next scene was complete chaos. Out jumped half of the legs, landing on the floor, the stove, Grandma and the table. As she picked each of them up, she cut the nerves and put them back in the pan. Eventually, she had the pan sizzling nicely, and no jumping legs.

I tried the frog legs that night to see what they tasted like, and really they tasted like chicken. The thing is, I don't like chicken either. I ate one bite, dropped the remainder in my lap and into my sock, and finished the meal quickly. Out I went into the yard, and I quickly threw the remainder of the leg over the hill. It would have been a serious problem if I had gotten caught, but I didn't.

Frog legs and I don't go well together, especially when it looks like there is life after death. It kind of put me off of anything that jumped for the moment.

THE OUTHOUSE

Many families in Pawhuska fished and hunted for meat to save money. I specifically remember one time a woman came to Grandma with a particularly delicate condition caused from being out in the woods.

This happened in the spring, when a woman came to Grandma dressed in the baggiest dress that I had ever seen. It was more like a sheet wrapped around her than any dress. She asked to discuss her "complaint" in private, and I went outside to entertain myself while the "doctor was in."

In about ten minutes I heard Grandma laughing so hard, I thought she was going to have a seizure. When that little lady laughed, her whole little body shook from her toes to her head. After another ten minutes, I saw the lady leave.

I went back inside and Grandma was still chuckling. I asked her what was up? She said that this woman had been in the woods for three days with her husband hunting and cleaning deer meat to smoke for the winter. Of course, during this time there were no outhouses available, and she had been using facilities between rocks as they moved around. Women need to sit through the whole procedure, where men don't, so it was just bad luck that this woman had picked two nice smooth boulders to sit on that had poison ivy growing between then. Yes, it was on her nether regions.

This was a particularly bad case, as she had been scratching, so now the rash was on her legs, arms and back. Of course, Grandma had to give her something pretty potent to do the job— so she had mixed puttyroot, mallow and sorrel for the sores and also mixed aloe, soapwort, and senega (or snake root) for the itching. She gave her some willow bark to brew in tea for inflammation and told her to come back if it did not clear up within a week. I had only seen her use puttyroot and mallow once before, because it was pretty strong stuff for sores, so I figured this poor woman must be in really bad shape.

I asked Grandma what she could have given her that would not have been so strong for the sores, and she told me that she preferred slippery elm, chamomile and Indian root most of the time.

This was a really busy summer. By my count, we treated over a hundred people for everything from gout to childbirth to skin irritations to varicose veins.

It was not long before it was time to go gathering again. I always enjoyed these trips because it was the time that Grandma and I had exclusively to ourselves to talk about healing and the Cherokee people's long use of nature and the eternal medicine cabinet.

This particular day was half over, when we went to a field we knew had good elderberry, as she was out of this and used it a lot for a variety of ailments. As we gathered the elderberry, she reflected on how her mother had taught her the healing ways. Of course, she had full-time training with her mother, but she said that with me, it was much the same, even though I was not there all of the time, because we "squashed time together" to get the most from it.

I reflect back now on our time together, and I see little things she did in her talks that stick with me: the pointing out of the medicine to be gathered with her wooden walking and digging staff, the tilt of her head as she viewed plants that would make the best mixtures, the way she held herself—proud, upright, and at ease with herself and the world around her. I often want to retrieve that feeling now in my hurried work day, but it only comes to me when I am out gathering medicines that I will be making myself. I guess it comes from Mother Earth, the abundance of the plants and flowers around me, and the oneness with nature.

LEARNING CHEROKEE
TSA LA GI DE GA DE LO QUA

Every summer, Grandma would take me outside, and we would have our Cherokee language lesson. She explained that our written language was unique, that Sequoyah had invented it just for the Cherokees, and it was important to learn it to preserve the culture. I told her I understood.

We usually went for a walk, and she would point to something and identify what she was pointing at in Cherokee and I would repeat it. I remember one day we were walking down a dirt road for our lesson, and she pointed at a spider and said (*ka-na-ne- s'gi*) and I would repeat it. We kept walking and a snake was on the side of the road and she said (*i-na-da*) and so on. If we started with animals, she tended to try to keep the subjects pointed to in the same category. That day we did animals. She would say:

so-qui-li	horse
s'qua-du-li	hornet
wa-ka	cow
sa -lo-li	squirrel
tsi-ya	otter

We would learn about ten to twelve words a day in the category that she chose, and the trick was to remember the words from day to day. She did not take kindly to me forgetting any word that she had taken the trouble to say, repeat and repeat again.

I asked her why she felt so strongly about learning the language, and she said that a healer needed to know the language because some plants and medicines were not identified in other vocabularies.

She also said that it was important to learn the language because many of the people that came to her were from the tribe and only spoke Cherokee, and she needed to know the language in order to understand what was wrong with them. She also needed to be able to tell them how to use the medicines for them to work.

I always got a mini-history lesson with each language walk and on this walk she told me about the seven clans of the Cherokee:

Ani sa ho ni	Blue Clan
Ani gi lo h	Long Hair Clan
Ani tsi s kwa	Bird Clan
Ani wo d	Paint Clan
Ani ka wi	Deer Clan
Ani ga to ge wi	Wild Potato Clan
Ani wa yah	Wolf Clan

She said that since we were from the Wolf Clan. Only people from this clan could kill a Wolf legally within the tribe, and she explained that many of the chiefs had come from our clan. She also said that it was forbidden to marry within our clan, that I would have to marry someone from one of the other clans. She said that this was a very old custom and still enforced by tribal law.

The red-and-white government was something else she mentioned that day. I asked what that was, and she said that the white government was in charge of the tribe during times of peace and prosperity and was made up of elders from the tribe. The red government was in charge during times of war, and she said that this government had not been in charge of the tribe since the relocation forced on Cherokees by the U.S. government. Since the red government was made of war chiefs, it would be hard for this to happen now, as there were no recognized war chiefs alive.

During these walks we often went five miles or more and did not even notice how long we walked. It was common knowledge when doing lessons that we would be home when we arrived.

She told me the number seven was sacred to the Cherokee people and that was why there were seven clans and seven festivals. I told her that I did not know of all of the festivals, and she said that was for another lesson.

She would walk and then speak into space as if seeing things that had happened long ago when she spoke Cherokee. Her mother spoke Cherokee, and she said she remembered hearing the oral stories of the Nation from her mother and grandmother while she was very young. She was the last of her immediate family alive, and sometimes I thought I could see her eyes tear as she spoke of the happiness she felt when with her brothers and sisters during a planting or during a festival. Every detail of her brothers and sisters was told, from appearance to personalities.

Since I wanted to know about her family, it was not hard to want to learn the language to know part of my history that was gone, but for her. The Cherokee alphabet was her first alphabet, and all 85 sounds were taught to me in the same sing-song tune for learning the English alphabet. She said she added the tune, so I could have a little memory help. She actually did not learn it that way.

During these walks I learned that the Cherokee traditions were passed through the female line, and she told me, in no uncertain terms, that she knew I would carry on this teaching with my daughters when they came. If I did not have daughters, then it would be my responsibility to let my sons know how the lineage and customs were to be learned, and then when they married, their wives would assume the role of head of teaching.

I often wondered why Grandma was such a strong woman in the face of adversity, outliving her family, her husband and seeing the culture disappear before her eyes. I asked once about this, and she looked me right in the eyes and said, "Remember who we are, where we came from, and what our Nation stands for. There is no excuse for lingering in the past, as the Creator had set the path of each person before they came into this world."

She was a person I looked up to wanted to be like, and I listened very hard to keep the knowledge alive that she shared. Now I am the last one in the family. I have no daughters or sons to pass this on to. These writings carry on the tradition of her wisdom and faith in the future.

STRAWBERRIES
A NI

Once I asked Grandma why she always had strawberries in her house—even during the winter. She told me it referred to a traditional Cherokee story about the beginning of the world (*ga lv la di e hi*) and the creation of first man and first woman. I asked her to tell me the story, and this is what she said.

First man and first woman were happy together, but sometimes, like all couples, they argued. Once they argued a long time, and first woman said she was leaving, not to return again. She started down a westward path through the forest and did not look back. Soon, first man began to miss her, and he followed after her.

The sun saw first man walking and asked him if he wanted first woman back, and he said yes. So to get first woman to stop walking down the path, the sun placed in front of her blueberries, which she stopped to eat. Then as she walked further, the sun caused blackberries to grow, and she stopped to eat.

As she walked further, first woman came to a berry she had never seen before. It was red and sweet with green leaves and white flowers. She stopped and ate one, and it was the sweetest and best berry she had ever eaten. After eating, she soon started missing first man, and she collected as many of these berries as she could and started eastward down the path toward first man.

Soon she found first man, and together they had the berries she had picked. These were strawberries and are a symbol of good luck and a reminder that it is useless to argue.

Grandma said she kept these in her home as a reminder of the first couple, and that a couple must work together for the good of the family and the good of the children. Each day, when she saw the strawberries, she remembered that even the first couple had argued, and that the strawberries were a reminder to her that she should count her blessings and not let the little things bother her in day to day life.

Today, I keep strawberries in my home year round, as a reminder that love is strongest when given the chance, to count my blessings and to honor the wisdom of my grandmother.

PICKING WALNUTS
SE DI DI NU TE SU GA

I have totally no sense of direction, and it is frustrating not to be
able to know which way is north, south, east or west. For the
longest time I thought I was the only one in my family with this
peculiar problem, but I soon found out my mother had it also.

Early fall was a good time to go to our favorite stand of black
walnut trees and pick up walnuts for Christmas. Every year dad
would twist and turn and drive and drive until we ended up in the
same small clearing in a wooded area, near Pawhuska, where the
walnuts were "ours." It was usual to dress in old clothes, with
boots, and we all carried old cloth sacks to gather in—gunny
sacks were best. They were light weight and strong.

This year was a cash crop of walnuts. There were so many on
the ground that we divided into groups for picking. Dad went
with my brother and grandfather, and Mom and I went with
Grandma.

If you have ever picked walnuts, you know that there is a lot
of talking, laughing, wandering around and just enjoying the fall
colors and weather. It is also hard work, and your back gets really
tired from bending and stooping. I guess we picked for about two
hours before our sacks were full, and we stood up, stretching our
backs, and started looking around. Nobody else was in sight, and
that was the days before cell phones.

That was when I learned that Mom did not know what
direction was what, just like me. I was thrilled I was not the only
one in the world without this knowledge. We both looked at
Grandma, who had a keen sense of direction. She said that she
reckoned that we were about a half mile from the others , north,
and she must have gotten blank stares from us, as she raised her
arm and pointed in a direction. All I could see around me were
trees, falling leaves, and walnuts. There was a hint of moisture in

the wind that day, and the cool breeze blew our hair around our faces, making us continually brush it back with our hands.

After Grandma pointed, we started walking along in that direction and occasionally picked up a walnut that looked particularly large and good. Sure enough, in about a half hour, we ran into the rest of our little group. I was happy to note that our sacks were full, where theirs were only half full. I could tell they had been telling hunting stories and reliving old times, because they were in the midst of telling a deer hunting story that I had heard at least four times.

As soon as they saw Grandma, however, walnut picking started in earnest. She walked up to them and said she was glad that they had already filled one sack and they were on their second sacks and that we would have to catch up. I snickered and looked at Mom—she had a twinkle in her eye also.

The goal of our picking was to get twelve sacks, as when the walnuts were cracked and picked there would be about four plastic bags full of nut meat that would be enough to go into cookies, cakes, fruit cake and heavenly hash that made up the part of the Christmas goodies Grandma made.

The guys started picking with haste, and soon we had our twelve sacks full of walnuts. It was time to head home, enjoy a meal, then start cracking and picking.

The cracking and picking was the hard part. If on the cracking team, soon your right hand and arm became sore from pushing down the cracker. If on the picking team, soon your fingers got sore and cut from the shell inside the outer shell surrounding the meat, and from picking through the mess. Even though we had little metal picks, it was a slow process and took quite awhile. However, this was all done with everyone participating, and this was where many memories were shared and stories told. If we were lucky, we would not miss any shells and get this in a cookie and break a tooth later on.

Picking was serious business. My brother and I were always pickers as smaller fingers made for better picking. I think that is why I really don't like walnuts today—too many sore fingers. As I look back on this time, I never remember watching television or listening to the radio—it was all family and talking and sometimes playing canasta for a whole day at a time.

The cooking part was great. Chocolate-chip cookies, sugar cookies, Russian nut balls, rum cakes, and fruit cakes all took turns baking as Grandma, Mom and I stirred and put together the next thing to go into the oven. The house smelled so good—like cinnamon, brown sugar, red-hots, fruits and mouth-watering chocolate. When we were finished, the whole kitchen table would be loaded down with the oven bounty. Of course, it could not be touched until Christmas Eve.

The next thing that we made, and it was my favorite, was heavenly hash. This was Grandma's baby, and she always made it. It was a mixture of many small pieces of fresh fruit, Jello, real whipped cream, and caramel. This was all whipped together and put in the fridge. After it set up, more whipped cream was added to the top with cherries to again be put in the fridge to set up. This dish had a special lead crystal bowl that it sat in, with just enough room for each layer. Anyone who touched that dish was toast if Grandma caught you. This was definitely Christmas day food, and it had always been that way. Many a greedy eye looked at that dish in the fridge, and one night Grandpa did the unforgiveable.

Christmas Eve day was full of activity, when we opened presents, said prayers (both traditional and Native), and ate the biggest dinner I ever remember. There were all of the goodies we had baked, and also a full ham baked with cloves and pineapple; real whipped mash potatoes; homemade rolls; corn-on-the-cob; green beans and ice tea. Usually after eating and washing up, everyone spread out to take a nap, play cards, read, or work on some project. Leftovers were the late meal, and it was come and get it in the fridge when you wanted to.

This Christmas Eve had gone well, and everyone was sleeping. Mom and Dad had the back bedroom, my brother and I shared the middle bedroom, and Grandma and Grandpa had the first bedroom by the front door. I will always remember the year, 1965, because that was the year Grandpa was nabbed red handed sneaking a spoonful of heavenly hash. I don't know how he was caught, because the first thing that woke me up was my Grandma calling someone a heifer at the top of her lungs and rattling off reasons why someone was in real trouble. When we found out it was Grandpa, we could all only keep out of the way and let things run their course.

Grandma started with a grumbling about the rules, how that was a special dish and didn't he know that it was for Christmas? He mumbled, with the spoon in his hand with whipped cream still on it, and Grandma then looked at the hash and saw that it had a dent in it! A dent! This was not allowed or tolerated.

She started revving up and got louder, and Grandpa shrunk and started walking backward. Things led to this and that and finally Grandpa started throwing napkins and cookies at Grandma to keep her at bay. That did it—she snapped, and started forward to grab Grandpa. I was hoping that he would last the night.

As she was coming for him, he started pulling stuff from the fridge to stop her—butter, pickles, and onions. All flew out and toward Grandma. As he threw each thing at her, she hauled off with her right foot, and kicked it and darn if it did not fly straight through the house and hit the front door each time. It was amazing—she should have been on a soccer team.

Eventually, this got a little more heated, and Grandpa knew he was cooked. My dad intervened and got them separated into corners, and Grandpa promised not to touch her special dish again. She accepted the apology quietly, too quietly I thought, and off everyone went back to bed.

The next day was Christmas, a special time for all of us. This was when we prepared the larger dinner of turkey, stuffing and all the trimmings, followed up with the heavenly hash. Everyone always saved room for the last dish, as it was only once a year that we got to taste it. Somehow that was Grandma's rule.

Everyone passed their plates to Grandma, and she gave heaping portions to everyone, and she knew every drop would be eaten. Everything from the night before seemed to be forgotten, and everyone dug in. It was about five minutes later when Grandpa let out a yelp and grabbed his mouth. It seemed he had gotten a thin piece of shell stuck between his front teeth.

Grandma said that these things happen and calmly held up a pair of pliers she had in her pocket. She went quietly over to Grandpa and used the pliers to pop that piece of shell right out. I am sure I heard her say something like "a lump of coal" as she walked back, but I could not be sure.

Everyone finished up, and all was well again with the Dawes clan. It was a tradition to sit on the porch for a while if not too cold and admire nature, but if too cold, to read to each other. I think most people chose their book for the season, and often an oral story or two would come alive from Grandma. I miss those Christmas get-togethers—but the memories are still strong.

DANDELION WINE
GI GA GE A DI TA S'DI

Grandma favored tinted glass jars and bottles for her home-made medicines, as many were sensitive to light. Also, I thought, all the colors looked very nice on her table.

One day Grandma had me picking dandelions in the yard. I thought she did not like them, as they were considered to be weeds, but she said all she wanted were the flowers. I asked the yellow part? She said that was all—no stems, no leaves, and no roots. I asked what she was going to use these for, and she said, "To make medicinal wine."

Soon I picked and picked and picked, my hands getting stickier all the time. I got about two big baskets full, and she said that was enough to start. To start? I was pooped.

She had a huge kettle on top of the stove, and in it she had about a gallon of water. To this water she added all of the dandelion flowers and brought them to a boil. Then she took the pot off the heat and covered it with a gauze rag. She said she would let it "rest" for a couple of days before proceeding.

After two days, she brought the mixture to a boil again and added sugar and oranges (no white from the oranges). Sometimes she would add raisins if she had some from commodities. She boiled this for about twenty minutes and then strained it through a cloth bag, and when it was cool, she added yeast to the mixture. This she poured into a large glazed clay crock and covered it loosely.

After a few hours she looked at it, and she just nodded to herself and started taking out colored glass bottles to pour the mixture into. She selected three large, pink-colored mason jars and poured them about three-fourths full. She then put them on the back porch to "cook." I could not see what she was cooking, as it was already cooked. She explained that wine has to age to be any good, and she had her standards to meet making this wine—it had to be clear and aged before anyone tasted it.

Having said this, she reached back behind a shelf and pulled out a blue-colored bottle that had a little dust on the top of it. It was corked, and the cork was held down by some wire that had been twisted around it. She got some pliers and cut the wire. She took a small jelly jar glass and poured about a teaspoon of it in the glass for me to taste. This was my first taste of any wine, let alone wine made with weeds my parents went to great lengths to kill.

Now not having tasted any kind of alcohol before, I thought you drank it right down, like soda, and that is what I did. After I stopped coughing, gagging and gasping for breath, I looked at Grandma. She smiled and said, "Turned out right good last year, huh?"

Well, I thought it tasted like gasoline smelled, so I made no comment. I just said, "It must be an acquired taste." She said, no, the more you drank, the better it tasted. I pondered on this for some time after we were finished cleaning up, but I could not understand why it would taste better the more you drank. It tasted awful!

Anytime she gave anyone some dandelion wine to soothe their nerves or to be sociable or whatever, I took note of what they did when they drank it. Everyone seemed to think it was the greatest thing since sliced bread. Everyone smiled, chatted and thanked her for her wine. I also noted that no one gagged.

The summer was going by fast now, and Grandma was running errands while my brother and I were supposed to go by a friend's house and collect some glass mason jars. The jar collecting did not take long, so we got bored. It was then I had a great idea. Why not try this year's wine a little just to see if my first taste had been faulty.

My brother was game, and in we went to the back porch to the pink-tinted mason jar that I had helped fill about two months before. We had a little trouble getting the wire off it, but were soon elated to see that we could just punch a hole in the cork and pour a little out into a glass to taste. We reasoned that no one would ever know a thing.

We got two jelly jar glasses from the cupboard and poured about an inch of the wine into the glass. It was pretty to look at—clear and kind of yellowish. I tentatively smelled it, and it still did not smell like something I would enjoy, but this was an experiment and sacrifices had to be made. We both took a slug of the stuff in our mouths.

My brother spewed his out of his mouth about two seconds after it touched his lips—covering me, the back porch wall, and part of the washing machine. While he was wiping that up, I decided to sip mine and see how that went. I took a little sip and another little sip, and sure enough, it was not as bad as I had remembered. I told my brother to sip his and see if he liked it that way. He took his first sip, and said, "It's crappy."

I said, "Take another sip; it seems to be better on the second sip." Well, he did and I did, and before we knew it, we had chugged back about two glasses worth.

It was strange, because when we went to stand up, everything kind of rolled around us, and we seemed not to be able to walk straight. We put that off to the porch being sloped, and we had been there for a while and were a little stiff. Also, everything was funny! There was not one topic we could mention that did not make us laugh: dead dog in the road (funny); we clogged the well up (funny); and on it went. We laughed and laughed, and it must have been a while, because before we knew it, we heard the front door open and knew Grandma was home.

Cripes! We had not resealed the mason jar yet, and looking around, we had moved stuff around while trying to walk. I could feel the dread creeping up in my bones when Grandma saw this mess.

My brother and I decided to make ourselves scarce and hide out by the barn until she calmed down—at least that was the plan. When my brother stood up, he fell back down, and we both started laughing again. Time meant nothing to us.

Grandma came in the kitchen, stood by the door, took things in, and knew at once we had been sipping the dandelion wine. She said later that it smelled like a bar in that kitchen that day. Anyway, instead of being mad, she laughed and said, "Now you both know why you should not drink—and tomorrow you will know even better why you should not drink." With that, she sent us to bed.

I could not believe how well I slept that night, even though the bed felt like it was rocking on the high seas. The next morning came, and as the first light came into my bedroom window, I found it hurt my head. In fact, my whole head hurt—a lot! Seeking out my brother, I found him in the bathroom throwing up and holding his head. That day was one of the most miserable we have ever spent, and Grandma never said another word about her dandelion wine.

The truth be told, I don't think I ever really drank more than one small drink in my life again, as I found out that I have a real intolerance for consuming alcohol—after two small drinks, that one time, I found out I laughed at everything, and woke up with a doozy of a headache.

I helped pick the dandelions again for Grandma next summer for that year's wine, but never again did I feel the urge to sip, taste, or otherwise imbibe any of her wine again. When we again filled jars next summer, she only smiled, and knew her wine was safe from me.

MY FIRST STOMP DANCE

My first stomp dance, that I really remember participating in, took place in Pawhuska, when I was about twelve years old. I had a new Cherokee dress, beaded moccasins made out of tanned deer hide, and a fringed shawl. I thought I looked "hot." I had seen stomp dances before, but Grandma had to be sure that I knew how to do the dance before she would let me in the circle.

My family arrived at the stomp dance ground. There was a huge bonfire burning in the center.. The rest was flat ground with grass and bales of hay lining the circle of the dance ring. The drummer began to beat, and even though a little nervous, the anticipation of participating in a real stomp dance overrode any shyness I had. I made sure my shawl was just so around my shoulders, and I dipped and walked with the beat of the drummers and singers. My grandmother explained that each loud beat of the drum was a sign to dip down toward Mother Earth, to give thanks for her abundance. I was mindful of this as I danced. Soon, many dancers—men, women, children—were all around me dancing around the ring. I felt a piece of the whole as we collectively joined in celebration together.

Grandmother stepped into the circle to dance on the third dance, and she too had the Cherokee dress, but much more ornate beading on her moccasins with a very old shawl that had been her mother's. The fringe from her shawl was much longer, and it flew in the air as she moved and dipped. I noticed the shadows of the dancers on the hay bales as we circled the fire, and I wondered if all people felt as I did then—renewed, full of the spirit that was Cherokee, and so very happy.

The dance went well into the night, and we took time out to eat the delicious fry bread being fried fresh and the roasted corn still in its husks.

I remember the bright stars, the bright colors, the rhythm of the dancers, the sound of the drum beat matching my heart. That night I became one with a larger community, a community older than I had ever been associated with. It stirred my blood, and I felt the bond of the Cherokees around me. Every time I dance, I relive the feeling of renewal and awareness that I am part of a larger family than just my immediate one—that of the Cherokee Nation.

RODEO TIME

While I was growing up, there was a rodeo and stock sale in Pawhuska each year. It was here that I met Ben Johnson, whose sister lived in Pawhuska; I met John Wayne; and I met Michael Landon of Bonanza fame. Ben was down visiting his sister, who was the county clerk, and Wayne and Landon were buying horses—Wayne a quarter horse and Landon a paint, but that is not the real story here.

Osage county has some of the best ranches and horses in the country—ask anyone from Pawhuska. Grandma often took the whole family to the rodeo to see the bronco riders and steer wrestling. Grandma knew a good horse and rider, and when the rider in the rodeo failed to live up to her standards, she would yell and holler that they better get back to Kansas, as they sure did not belong in Osage County. Now Osage County is the reservation of the Osage Native Americans, and the only reservation in Oklahoma. Many of those riders were Native Americans— and she knew it. She also knew that telling them they were doing less than the best made them mad. You see, Grandma reveled in a good "up front and personal" confrontation once in a while. She said "It makes the blood move faster and cleans out the pipes."

One day, after this yelling and hollering, two riders ended up in the Osage Bar playing shuffleboard. Shuffleboard was a favorite of mine, as those round metal pucks were heavy and slid real nice down that flat black board lined with saw dust. Grandma had a sign above the bar that said, "Trouble makers will not be tolerated—the management," which she had painted herself on a spare board from the back.

The bar was about to open, so my brother and I left, as we were still minors. We saw the two cowboys come in the front door and order a beer. They looked at my grandmother closely, but she did not seem to notice. Well, we both decided to watch from outside through the back window to see what was going to happen, because we knew that Grandma had seen those old boys eyeballing her.

Eventually, the dudes had about four beers tucked under their belts and noticed that she looked like the gal that heckled them during the riding events. They confronted her, and we saw her lips move and she said something about "*di tli hi*" (warrior) and "heifer" and the poop hit the sandbox. As the dudes came around the bar after her, she walked to the shuffleboard table, grabbed a puck, and took aim with one eye shut, arm cocked —fired.

The puck hit the first dude right between the eyes and cold cocked him flat to the floor. As his friend continued toward her, she reached for the other puck and shut the one eye and stared down the pike five by five at him. He stopped dead in his tracks, looked at his buddy on the floor just coming to, and politely said he would be leaving with his friend.

She reminded him to pay up, and they left a $50.00 bill on the counter. She was smug the rest of the night.

BLUESTEM LAKE

V DA LI

Blue Stem Lake was a small lake outside of Pawhuska that had
land for cattle to graze on, wheat fields, and some houses around
it. It had a multitude of cattle guards that used to bump my
brother and me almost out of grandpa's old '56 Chevy pickup as
we rolled over them. We often went around the lake, and it was
called "going around the circle." I never knew why it was called
that, as we did not go in a circle, but a wavy line that ended up on
the far edge of Pawhuska by the Dairy Queen, but it was always
called that in my family.

On these trips the grownups sat in the pickup cab, and my
brother and I sat in the back of the truck's bed. Often we went at
dusk, and it was always fun trying to dodge the flying bugs
buzzing around our heads and slamming into the pickup bed as
we went our fast 25 miles an hour (as fast as grandpa deemed
safe). Much laughing and slapping was done by my brother and
me as we held on to the sides of the truck and sat on the wheel
wells above the tires.

On these trips we often would stop and look at a particular
view, or a new dock being built, or the height of the water on the
old cement water stick in the lake. One of these stops particularly
sticks in my mind. My brother was four and I was six.

This day had been very warm, and going around the circle was
a way to cool off and to get minds off of having no air
conditioning. Grandpa said we had "4-80" air-conditioning in the
truck. When I asked what that meant, he said, "Four windows
and eighty miles an hour," and would snicker. Anyway, we
stopped by a friend's dock that was in disrepair. It had once been
a glorious dock that had a walkway with rails to hold onto. It was
wooden and once had a nice framed a little boat house on it. Now
the dock was a shell of its former self, what I would now call

"barely floating." But, always having the fishing tackle in the truck, we decided to dig some worms and try our luck.

I always fished a tight line—meaning a string that was tied on to a piece of branch that was handy with a hook and sinker on it. The touch of my forefinger on the string could feel the vibrations of a fish nibbling at the hook, and I had surprising luck with catching crappie, sun fish and small bass. My brother always fished with a cane pole, and my parents and grandparents always fished with "real" poles with wind-up string.

I often explored the lake shore during these stops and nearly always got into some trouble, much like I do now. I was a magnet for misadventure.

This time I stepped on a snake that was as thick as my arm and longer than my leg. Needless to say, I angered the snake, and it took out after me, but I could run in those days like I was on fire. Screaming at the top of my lungs, I ran back toward the dock, about twenty feet away, with the snake hot on my heels. I ran down the ramp to the dock. One of the rotten boards collapsed. I fell through and landed flat on my butt in the lake.

I was not worried about drowning at first, because all I could think about was the snake. I felt a whooshing noise above me and looked up just in time to see one foot of my grandmother flying down the ramp toward the shore. Evidently she had seen the snake and was after it. As she flew by all I could hear was some Cherokee and the word "heifer" and I knew that snake was not long for this world.

Since I now knew that the snake was not going to get me, I noticed that my feet could not touch bottom, and drowning because a serious threat. Just as I was going down for the second time, grandmother's hand yanked me up through the walkway and onto the dock—in one smooth movement. Her adrenalin must have been pumping hard, because she still had a large branch clutched in her right hand with blood on it. Needless to say, the snake had met his end.

I started to thank her as I sputtered water and tried to tell my story, but her calling me a "heifer" brought me up short. I knew I was in the deep, deep doo-doo, and I started shaking.

I was ready for a paddling, but all she did was hug me and start crying and telling me that I was going to be the death of her. She was mad, happy, tired and squishing the hell out of me. I thought it better not to tell her that she was hugging too tight.

My parents later told me that they had never seen her go so fast. It was like a heartbeat to heartbeat that she got the snake, got me, and got me in a hug. She always claimed that I was a magnet for trouble, and she was right, I still have that same problem. But I don't go exploring lake shores on my own now either.

MAMMA SKUNK
DI LI

My grandma had a reverence for all life, including wildlife. She only killed what was needed to feed her family in the early years, and only then with a prayer and thankfulness to the animal that had sacrificed its life. This belief extended throughout her years.

Grandpa had another idea about varmints—if they ate crops, disrupted his yard and flowers, cut down trees, or otherwise put a glitch in his usual routine—they had to go.

Once summer day Grandma and Grandpa had a serious disagreement about a skunk that was living under the front porch with her brood of tiny newborns. Grandpa was all for "doing them in" and Grandma was arguing that they were not hurting anything and "live and let live."

I knew that something was going to give, because Grandpa's stubborn streak matched my grandmother's.

So it came to pass that a day later, as Grandma was hanging out the washing in the back yard and I was helping her, we heard a yelling commotion coming from the front yard but could not tell what was happening. The sound seemed to come and go. We ran around to the front of the house, and there was Grandpa with mamma skunk clutched in his hand, going around and around in circles on the lawn, yelling like a wild man. Evidently, he had tried to grab mamma, or baby, by the tail and haul it out, and mamma had clamped her sharp teeth on his right hand and now would not let go of him. So there he was, with mamma skunk chomping on his right hand, and him swinging her around and around trying to get free. Grandma yelled at him to, "Drop that skunk !" but I really don't think he had much control at this point.

It was a one in a million sight to behold: Grandpa in his seventies, yelling and cussing, and mamma skunk's tail proudly up in the air going around and around with him. I don't believe that I have seen anyone whirl around that fast for so long.

Now, Grandma's advice might have worked, except for the small complication. Mamma finally got mad enough to spray as she went around and around, and each whirl brought more fragrance into the air and around the house. Grandpa got madder and madder.

The stalemate was broken after about what seemed five minutes when Grandpa recovered some of his wits and used his left hand to pry mamma off his right hand. Mamma let go, hit the ground on four feet, and the minute she hit, turned tail and unloaded the whole shebang right on Grandpa. I have never smelled anything so foul from that day to this. After unloading, mamma skunk calmly waddled off and wiggled back under the porch. Grandpa was still yelling, cussing a blue streak, and I do believe he slurred her ancestry at least once, maybe twice.

Grandma was disgusted, reminded him of her philosophy, and told him to strip off all of his clothes, including shoes, and go to the creek and wash up. He complained that the creek was cold and someone might see him. She told him that no one was interested in seeing his wrinkled old body, and besides, everyone would stay upwind from him because of the overpowering skunky smell. Off Grandpa went to the creek, muttering and dragging his feet, and he did not come back until after dark. He later told me he now knew what Adam felt like before the fig leaf came into play.

While waiting for Grandpa to return, Grandma was busy opening up all of the tomato juice she could find and squashing all of the fresh tomatoes from the garden. She filled a wash tub with these in the back yard and left a big cardboard sign in the front that he was to *wash again* in the tomato juice for at least one hour. She lit her smallest lantern for him to see by. It gave off a fireflies' glow. She was that mad at him.

Finally, Grandpa banged on the back porch door about 9:00 p.m. He wanted to be let in as he said he was sick of tomatoes and did not want to see one the rest of his natural life. To her credit she let him in, but boy did he still stink! While she tended to his hand, I was busy tying a dish cloth around my face to cover my nose to save it more indignity and hoping to get some air once in a while.

After doctoring Grandpa with a poultice Grandma put him in a bed on the screened in front porch and said he could dry out there, and possibly kill some mosquitoes while he was at it with the stink.

I had to leave for home the next day, but I hear that Grandpa spent the better part of the summer sharing the top side of the mamma's home. Just goes to show that Grandma was right—live and let live, or get skunked with payback.

COYOTE

WA YA

Often Grandma would tell traditional Cherokee stories to me, but usually to make a point when I had done something stupid. One story that she told, more than once, was about the trickster, Coyote.

I have heard many variations on this since she told me the story, but this reflects the way she told the story:

One day a rich man came to Coyote and asked him to sell him the deer Coyote had in his pen to eat, as he did not want to go to the trouble to hunt one for himself. Coyote quickly agreed, and traded a great deal of money for the deer, which he had on his back with the feet tied.

Coyote saw a way to make more money and went ahead of the man and on the trail left his left shoe. As the man went by, he saw the shoe, but thought one shoe would do him no good. The man went on along the trail. Coyote was still ahead of the man and left his right shoe on the trail for the man to find. As the man found the right shoe, he thought to himself he should have taken the left shoe, as now he would have a new pair of shoes. So, he lay the deer on the ground and went back for the right shoe.

While the man was going back for the right shoe, Coyote took the deer and put it back into his pen. When the man came back for his deer, he assumed that it had escaped, and decided to return to Coyote to see if he had any more deer he could buy.

Of course, when the man got to Coyote's house, he saw a deer in the pen. He asked Coyote if he could buy this deer as he had lost his other deer. Coyote agreed, but said that this was his last deer and would cost double. The man agreed, and Coyote made double the money off one deer sold twice to a lazy man.

Grandma used this story when I had been a little slow in doing what she asked of me, or I had found something else to look at or play with. She told me that no good comes from not working and learning for oneself. Others could take advantage of my stupidity if I let them, and if I let them, I deserved it. After about twenty times, I learned to avoid the error of my ways and also avoided the story, which by now was irksome to hear. It only meant that I had been lazy again, and needed to be reminded that these were not the ways of life. Life came at a price, and learning was part of that price. Besides, I really hated to be called "stupid" and listen to such a long story, knowing I could have avoided it.

THE TRAIL OF TEARS: A LEGACY

One Sunday afternoon, my parents, brother, and I were invited
over to lunch at my Cherokee great-grandmother's home. She
lived in a three-story big white house on the on the outskirts of
Pawhuska. I am not sure how old I was, but I have many images of
this meeting. The first image was that my brother and I played in
the yard a long time while dinner was prepared. She had chickens
and ducks, and I remember shutting up my brother in a chicken
coop and not letting him out for the better part of a half an hour.
The coop was none too clean, and he was distinctly unhappy.

Of the house, I remember the parlor: the old braided red rugs,
the lace on tops of the chairs my great-grandmother had tatted,
the horsehair couch and chairs to match in red with very dark
wood trim, the shelf that ran around the top of the high ceiling
room that had many dolls of such color and shape that I stared in
awe at their beauty. I found out later these were dolls that my
great-grandmother had collected over her lifetime, and many were
antique. She showed me one with a beautiful pale blue dress,
which had layers and layers of lace petticoats, a porcelain head,
black silk curly hair, and arms and hands that looked real. I
remember this doll, as I still have it. She gave it to me that day to
remember her by.

Next to the parlor there was a great room that held a large
rectangular heavy wooden table with twelve chairs around it. The
tablecloth was white, and it was lace. The plates were white with
little blue cornflowers around the rims, and the glasses were
heavy and had a crystal decoration.

The best thing about the visit, though, was getting to talk
with my great-grandmother, as I understood she had been ill, and
this was one of the first days she had been able to see me. She
called me to her as she sat in a massive overstuffed blue chair, and
I sat on her knee. She looked very old to me, but she had my

grandmother's face and eyes. She smiled and talked to me of many things including: how she had lived her life, tales of the Cherokee Nation, the importance of learning the way of the tribe, and the story of her mother's mother and the trail of pain that she had walked. Later, I learned that she spoke of the Trail of Tears. This is what she told me of that time:

> It was winter she spoke of. She said that many women and children were being walked to a place far away by the army. Her mother told her that promised food never came, and relentless walking killed many woman and children who either froze, starved, or were killed when they fell. She spoke of the abuse by the soldiers of the women, and how many tribes were in this march, not just the Cherokees. Each day they would start at daylight, walk all day, and drop where they were when the soldiers told them to halt—she said it was a journey that had the sounds of crunching feet, the crying of women and hungry children, the smell of death and hopelessness. Men of the tribes were treated very harshly, and if they tried to protect a woman or child, were killed or beaten.

Her words were so foreign to my young mind that it was not until my grandmother told me the story again later, that I came to really understand the suffering and hardship so many went through during that long walk.

Although I thought my great grandmother told the story as a tale, I knew it was more, much more, even as young as I was then—around eight or nine.

When I was sixteen, my grandmother gave me a scrap of tanned hide that had once been part of a bag that had held small things and usually was attached to a woman's dress. She said this scrap was from my great-great-grandmother's mother's pouch she wore during the walk. I cried when she gave it to me, and as I held

it. I still cry when I hold it now. That fragile piece of hide, as rough
and stained as it is, allows me to visualize the woman who was my
ancestor once again, struggling to survive so the tribe would
endure.

My grandma said I now had a legacy, a legacy to let people
know of the truth of what our people suffered and endured.
Because we survive today shows that we had the strength to still
hear those who suffered for us.

THE BEADS OF BONE

KO LA

One day my grandma gave me a necklace (*a-ya tli- di*) that was
made up of tiny beads that were round, but thick with holes in the
middle of each one. The necklace, when on, went around my neck
one hundred times.

She told me that this was a bone necklace made by her mother
for her, and she was passing it on to me to take care of until I
passed it on to another in the family. Each bead was almost the
same off-white color, the same size (about pencil eraser size) and
had varying sized holes through the middle of them. She said that
it was buffalo (*ya-na-sa*) bone, and had come from many buffalo
and had taken many years to complete. It was used in ceremonies
of celebration and honor. The beads were hung together on a
yellow waxy string, which looked like it was darkened in some of
its length. She said it was sinew, a natural string that was dried
from the ligaments of the buffalo.

I have now had the necklace for over 35 years, and even
though I thought it would need to be restrung sometime, it never
has broken. I have only worn it once, and that was to honor my
grandmother's passing to our ancestors, and since then it has been
kept lovingly in the cardboard box that she gave me.

I have often wondered how many women of my line helped
make that necklace and how many cut the bone, drilled the holes,
and dried the sinew that the beads are strung on. I touch them
and feel a great pride and honor that I was given them. Someday,
soon, I will be passing them on to another in my line to cherish
and care for, with these stories, so that they too, will know what
they represent and the message they hold. They represent *u-du-gi-
gv-di* (hope).

BEAD WORK

Learning beadwork was not as fun as I thought it would be. I begged Grandma to show me how she made such beautiful jewelry, hair combs, and borders. Finally, after about three years of begging, she agreed to show me, but I would have to agree to complete a piece if she started one with me. I very swiftly agreed—my first mistake.

The day finally came, and she had me follow her to the back bedroom where her beads, needles, and threads were stored. I was overwhelmed with the number of strings of bright beads. Some were faceted, some were plain, some were multi-colored, and some were clear, but tinted. In her boxes she had various threads, needles, buckskin, pins and loose beads of all colors. I had good eyes then, and even then, the beads were tiny—about the size of a wheat kernel.

She asked me what I wanted to make, and I said a simple necklace. She then asked what pattern, and had I considered how long, what type of beads, or anything else? I said I would let her pick—my second mistake. You see, my grandmother believed that if you were going to do something right, you should start with something hard, and then everything else would be easy. A view I came to not share.

She told me that she recommended we do a star pattern and use five types of beads, and it should be at least fourteen inches in length. Not knowing what I was getting into, I said yes. My third mistake.

She pulled out an empty tray and started putting beads of every kind in slots in the tray. She arranged a spool of waxed string, pins, and one smooth stone of garnet. She drew me a picture of what the pattern looked like, demonstrated twice how to do it, and said all of the beads in the tray would be gone when the necklace was finished. I asked about the garnet stone, and she said this was to put in the middle of the necklace, and I would have to drill a hole through it. She told me drilling the hole would come last. It seemed straight forward.

The next day I started the necklace five times, and still I could not get the pattern right. I broke the string three times. I was going blind looking at all of those teeny tiny beads. I began to see I might have gotten myself into a tight fix. I decided to ask Grandma for help, at least in starting the thing.

So the next day dawned, and after chores, I asked Grandma if she could help me start the necklace. She said, "Child, if you want to really learn how to do things you must learn to stand on your own two feet." I took that as a no.

I was determined that I would get this thing done by the end of the summer, and I alternated in emotions from pain, suffering, joy, bliss, anger, and extreme frustration. Ultimately, I did finish the necklace; however, there were several beads left in the slots in the tray, and I was terrified that I had done something wrong. I checked the pattern several times, the tension of the string, and the color of the beads three times. It was fourteen inches and I still had beads left!

Grandma would ask occasionally how things were going with the beadwork throughout the summer, and I always told her, "It's going," and left it at that. Now it was the end of the summer, and the day came when Grandma asked to see my necklace and what I had accomplished during the long hours beading in the back room.

I got the necklace, and before showing it to her I said, "I really, really tried, but I think that something may be wrong as I have just a few beads left on the tray." She asked how many beads were left and I side-stepped it by saying, "A few." Grandma was no fool, far from it, and she knew I was hedging. She just said, "Let's see the necklace."

I held my breath as she took the necklace and turned it over and over in her old hands, running her long, slender fingers along the beads to see if they were even and straight. She paid special attention to the star pattern and how it looked, making sure each point was exactly matched with the other points of the star. I was about to faint from holding my breath when she finally spoke. She said, "For a first try, it is tolerable." I could have screamed with joy. Coming from her, this was a very good compliment. She could have said, "Do it over."

Then she said, winking at me, "I always had a few beads left over too, but I wanted to keep you on your toes." I was too excited to be mad and gave her the necklace as a gift for teaching me the way to bead. She seriously thanked me, and said that she would wear it in honor.

This was the way my grandmother imparted wisdom. She believed that by doing, a person learned through their experience.

I have only beaded a few times since then, as the tiny beads are tinier now, and my hands are slower. But I still think of her smiling face, her brown hands holding my necklace, and the pleasure she took in accepting my first beadwork.

MY FATHER:
GRANDMOTHER'S STORIES
E DO DA

My father was the oldest of Grandma's four children. He was very agile, and he was once offered a job with Barnum and Bailey for tightrope walking. But there are other stories that my grandmother tells me that my father never admitted to me when I asked him.

My father was only 5'8", thin and pure muscle. He was small in high school, as the neighboring Osage guys tended to be big-boned and tall. Grandma said that he was never picked on though, because he had two large Osage friends that he always ran around with, and if someone got really nasty to him, one of his friends would squeeze the offending party until they passed out. I believe Grandma was actually proud that her boy stood up for himself. He was the Band Major in high school, and I know, from talking with his many friends, he was well respected and smart. He became the first of Grandma's children to graduate from college with honors—Oklahoma State University.

Grandma said that he was a handful growing up, though. She spoke of the time that the family was working in their large garden in the hot sun. They had been working for about two hours, and it was well over 100 degrees. My father would have been about ten.

She said all of a sudden, she heard him cry out and drop like a rock into the dirt. She was terrified, and even though he weighed close to what Grandma did, she carried him up to the house and laid him on the bed, ready to administer any medicine he might need. As she started to give him some water with "Black Draw" in it, he jumped up off the bed and said that he just got hot and did not want to work in the garden anymore. Grandma got mad and made him stay under her four poster bed for two hours as punishment.

She said that about an hour later, she went in the house with fresh vegetables and noticed some smoke coming from the front room. She went in there and saw that it was coming from the bedroom and specifically under her bed. She looked under and saw that my father had lit a small pile of matches under the bed. She hauled him out and asked him what he thought he was doing. She still remembered that he calmly said, "I got cold, so I lit a fire." I am not sure what punishment that got him, but the story is still told in the family.

Another story was when my father got mad at his older sister for making him take the blame for one of her pranks. Well, Grandma said that night my father went out the back door and moved the outhouse over about two yards so that the hole it usually sat over was exposed. In the dark his sister went to the outhouse that night and fell in the hole. To hear it told, she raised quite a commotion. No one would tell me what happened after that, but I bet the s—t hit the fan.

Another time dad and a friend were digging a cave for themselves on the steep side of the hill by the house, and it was hot and dirty work. Grandma said that a guy came by and asked what they were doing. My dad said that they were digging for treasure that they had buried there two years ago, and he should go away so that could get on with it. The guy begged them to let him help, but they said no, he had to go. They decided to go into the house for lunch then, but told the guy again, not to touch a thing. The guy swore he wouldn't.

Grandma said from the house's front window, my dad and his friend watched this guy dig and dig and dig in the hot sun for that treasure—only to leave about two hours later without a thing. That was when dad and his friend went back out. She said he had a really good cave dug, and that it was used later to store some fruits.

My dad is gone now, but his love and prankish stories still live on. He would probably deny these happened, but Grandma swore they did—I think I believe her.

WHEAT HARVEST
U TSA LE S'DI

My grandparents, for a time, were custom cutters who traveled from Oklahoma up to South Dakota to cut fields of wheat. Grandpa used to drive the combine, and Grandma would drive the truck by the combine as it unloaded. My father took his turn driving the truck to the elevator as the two trucks took turns carrying wheat.

Harvest is a very hot, sweaty and buggy time. When my brother and I were smaller, we would be in the bed of the large trucks shoveling the grain down to the end of the truck as the combine unloaded it from the funnel. It is amazing how many bugs, grasshoppers, mice, and other varmints get caught up in the grain dump. It was also our job to get the mice out of the grain as we saw them. Usually there were not too many, and mostly dead. Even though we were young, in good shape, and nearly tireless, the heat, dust of the crop, and trying to stay upright in the wheat as it was dumped all took a toll. Often, when we went home in the evening, only our eyes and teeth were fairly white. The rest of our bodies were covered with dust and grit from head to toe.

During one harvest I went with my father to the elevator in the truck and remember being very hot—which meant it was about 110 degrees, as I really did not notice heat that much in my teens. He had water in a jug in the truck, and when we got to the elevator, the elevator man gave me a tiny salt block, about the size of a child's toy wooden block, to suck on. I asked my father what this was for, and he said it was to help retain water and not get dehydrated. So while the truck was weighed and dumped, I stood by the shade of the elevator and felt very grown up sucking my salt block and watching the lines of trucks waiting for their grain to be unloaded.

When back at the field, the other truck was being loaded and anyone not working would sit under the empty truck in the wheat field, in the only shade for miles and try not to move so no extra body heat was generated. I could actually see the heat waves rising from the ground as we sat in the field. It took about five days to do six fields of wheat, and if the wheat was "downed" from hail or rain, it took longer, as the combine had a special pick up fork that had to be used when cutting, and the combine had to go slower.

I found out early on that combines can only go a certain speed or the tail fan gets clogged up with straw, and unclogging a tail fan is really not fun and takes hours. I know this, as Grandma let me drive the combine for ten minutes and, yep, I clogged that baby right up. Grandpa was fit to be tied, but Grandma said I would remember not to do that again. She was right—I never messed the tail fan up again because Grandpa would not let me drive the combine again. That really did not bother me, as combines then were hot and noisy and a real pain to steer—but I never let him know that.

As I grew older, my brother and I could drive the trucks and go to the elevators to dump the grain while others worked in the fields. This gave them time to rest and take a cooling-off break from the heat.

When I was in school and could no longer get the time off to help, my grandparents always gave my brother and me a silver dollar from every wheat harvest they did, and we ended up with 45 silver dollars each when they retired. I still have most of those dollars, and they are now proudly in special holders in a notebook on my bookshelf. I have only to look at them to see the faces of my parents and grandparents and brother—of course I see them with the sweat, dirt and grit. I see us together—something that has been taken away from me with the years. I am the only one remaining from those happy times.

My parents were probably in their early thirties then, which would have made my grandma and grandpa about 50-something, but anything older than me was "old," and I did not think much about it at the time. It is only on reflection that I see how young my parents, brother and grandparents were when I actively participated in the harvest. I am now approaching sixty, and I see with wonderment the youthful faces in my memory compared to the pictures I have of everybody's later years.

NOODLING
DI GA LV NV HI

When I was about eight and my brother about five, Grandma had
some great fish fries. I had always admired the biggest fish caught,
because they were whoppers. I finally asked the guy who brought
in a ten-pound catfish how he had caught it—he said he noodled
for it. For the life of me, I could not see how anyone could catch a
fish with a noodle and told him so. He laughed and said that to
noodle was to put your hand under rocks and feel for the fish and
grab it by the mouth and catch it. This seemed pretty easy, and I
asked Grandma to take my brother and me noodling at the creek
someday. She said she would think about it. I figured she never
would, as she could not swim.

But I was in for a surprise. The next day Grandma suggested
my brother and I go with her to the creek to look for minnows for
fishing the next day. In those days, it was easy to get a little net
and with one person on one end, and another on the other end,
scoop up and herd minnows into the net in shallow water. It was
simple, especially if there was a tiny inlet where each person could
stay on dry land while scooping.

We got a bucket full in no time, and we kids wanted to learn
how to noodle. Grandma was hesitant, partly because she would
have to get in the water to demonstrate, and partly because it
could be somewhat dangerous. She explained that lots of things
live under rocks—but we would not hear of it. We were stupid
and brainless as I look back, but kids have a way of making danger
fun. Her stronger will did not prevail that day, and she
demonstrated on land what to do.

One should wade into shallow water, get a firm stance, and
start using a hand to feel under rocks. When a mouth of a fish was
felt, we should grab it and bring it to the surface. Several problems
arose from this: the stones in shallow water were very slippery

with moss. My brother and I got dunked several times before getting a "firm stance" after Grandma pulled us up spitting and coughing. However, we were determined, and finally we stood rooted in the middle of a shallow inlet in Bird Creek, just under the bridge, where there was lots of sand and standing water in side pockets of rock.

I went first, being the dumbest, to start feeling around under several big rocks to see what I could find. For the longest time, I could only feel mud, rough rock, moss and absolutely no movement at all. I asked Grandma what a fish mouth would feel like, and she said, "You can't mistake it." I later could swear she had a little smile on her face.

My brother, in the meantime, was on the other side of the inlet trying his luck. He too, had no luck in finding any fish, let alone the big one.

On and on we went, for over an hour, with me finding a firm stance in another spot, and dipping my right hand in the water to my elbow trying to find the illusive huge fish. I was getting hot, sweaty, and the flies were eating me alive, but I did not want to gripe or quit. I moved again to another spot closer to the bank and started my boring bending, and dipping to the elbow.

I was going to try my luck under a big boulder that jutted out over the water and down into it further on. I started creeping around with my fingers, and felt something move. But after waiting for a few minutes with fingers poised, I felt nothing. So I continued moving my fingers side to side now to see if I could get a grip on old grumpy that was hiding down there.

I had no sooner started wrangling my fingers back and forth, and something bit down on my right hand with a vengeance. I let out a whoop and started dancing like my pants were on fire—the damned thing would not let me go. I knew I was going to lose that hand, and that was the one I wrote with too. I had visions of learning to write again with my other hand, as the monster continued to grip and chomp down on my fingers.

Soon, my fingers starting going numb. Grandma came over, wading as fast as she could through that mossy bed of a creek, and eventually got to my side. She reached in and grabbed my right arm and commenced to tug and tug—but my hand still would not come free. By now, my brother had a grip on Grandma's other arm and they both commenced to pulling. All the while, I was yelling and screaming and dancing the jig. It seemed like an hour, but Grandma said it was about ten minutes, before up popped my hand and attached to it was the biggest catfish I had ever seen.

Did anyone know that catfish have teeth? Well, they don't— but they sure as hell have a mouth of "steel" that can clamp down like a vise. Over went my brother and Grandma and me into the water, and me with that damn fish still attached to my hand.

I was sitting in the shallow water, hammering the fish's head as hard as I could with the most convenient instrument —a small rock. Grandma said I sounded like a warrior on the warpath the way I yelped, screamed, twitched, splashed, and whammed that fish. The damn thing *still* would not let go.

Grandma got things in hand and told my brother to grab the tail of the fish, and she would smack it with a branch she had found on the bank. He held the fish, she started to bring down that branch with a mighty swing, and just as it hit the fish, the branch broke. I guess it was rotten.

It was then she started speaking in Cherokee (the words she would not teach me), making gestures, and turning red. She grabbed that fish by the gills and yanked it so hard, it let go and she went flying about three yards before she hit the water with a whoosh. Down under the water she went, and she popped up like a cork almost as soon as she went down. She still had a hold on the fish! God bless her anyway. I was going to have the pleasure of eating that good-for-nothing!

She waded to shore, dragging the flopping fish, my brother and me. I was in shock, as I did not even feel my hand until I got to shore and started looking around. I looked at my right hand, and two of the fingers were bent at a real funny angle, kind of like a door had slammed on them As soon as I saw that, they started hurting like a "son a bitch." Of course, Grandma did not hear me thinking these words, or she would have had some Indian story to tell me about how stupid I was.

She bagged the fish, and we all went up to her house and she weighed it. The fish weighed in at twelve pounds and was as long as my leg.

Another thing that people should be told about noodling is that catfish whiskers are really sharp and hurt even more when they jab into your hand than just the bite.

Things started moving quickly then: Grandma straightened my fingers quickly. I peed my pants. She yanked out a piece of fish whisker. I screamed.

She cleaned my injuries, put some herbs on them, and bound them up in a splint. She must have given me some valerian root, because the next thing I knew, it was dinner time.

I crawled out of bed, managing to keep thoughts to myself about my aching hand, and saw to my delight that old Death Grip was the main dish. As we sat around the table, Grandma said that we could noodle tomorrow if we wanted. We both almost shouted "no" at the same time. I reasoned that I needed to keep at least one hand in working order.

We dined richly that night— great fish, hot corn bread, and lots of real butter. I got my revenge. Of course the fish was fried in bacon grease and corn meal. I can hear my arteries clog now as I tell the story.

The next day, we all took the minnows that we had gathered and fished at Blue Stem off the bank for whatever had the mind to grab our hooks. I got to thinking that this must have been real hard on people who had to noodle to catch fish this way all of the time. Grandma said that was why bone hooks were invented as well as nets. I do believe she was enjoying the moment—not saying "I told you so," but one of those looks that grownups always give kids when they are chuckling on the inside and bursting to say it. My brother and I both knew that look.

That was the first, and last time that we ever went noodling. It was after this little incident that Grandma said we were lucky. Sometimes snapping turtles liked to hide under rocks also. I have seen a snapping turtle bite an inch diameter stick and break it in two—and started thinking what a twit I had been for wanting to noodle. Now I knew why they called it noodling—that is all you got back after you got your hand caught and half ripped off.

THREE ON A COLUMN

When I was fourteen, Grandma asked grandpa to teach me how
to use a standard shift, because so many cars were now automatic.
Grandma had purchased a '56 Chevy pickup brand new off the lot
for $3,000.00, and it still looked brand new. She reasoned that it
had three gears on the column, and I could learn just fine from
this.

It was a fine spring morning when Grandpa, my dad and my
brother (in the back of the pickup) started out for the big lesson.
Grandpa took the truck down to the cemetery, where it was flat,
and he reasoned that everyone there was dead, so I couldn't kill
them again. I was slightly aggravated that he thought so little of
my motor control. However, he demonstrated how to shift from
first gear, and up to second gear, and back down and over for third
gear. Reverse, he said, was up and toward me. I looked forward to
this, as I had seen people shift all of my life, and it seemed like a
snap.

After showing me all he could while stopped, Grandpa moved
over by my father and told me to get behind the wheel. I was more
than excited. This was going to be fun!

I slammed the door of that old truck and put my foot down on
the clutch and my right foot on the brake as told. Now Grandpa
got really serious and said, "Let the clutch out really, really, really
easy." Okay, I could do easy, I thought. With the left foot on the
clutch and right one on the brake, I pulled the shift lever down
and toward me to get it into first. Grandpa said, "Give it a little
gas as you let out the clutch, and she will go just fine."

So I gave it a little gas, and popped that clutch out, and the
truck jumped a couple of times and the motor croaked. Silence in
the car met my puzzled look. Grandpa again said, "Let the clutch
out easy" and told me to try it again.

It was a good thing we were in the cemetery, because I jumped and croaked the truck all over the place and even nicked one of the stones trying to stop. Grandpa was turning a funny purple color, but Dad said, "She will get it in time, and Grandma wants her to learn."

Grandpa looked at my dad, and then he looked at me and said, "Let the clutch out REALLY easy and she will go just fine." I let that clutch out as easy as I could several times, and each time the truck jumped. My brother, in the back, had learned to sit down in the bed for safety, and I killed that engine quicker than squashing a bug.

After about two hours of jumping and croaking, I finally got it into my head that you don't have to let the clutch all the way out for the truck to go—just ease up on it a little at a time. Hallelujah, I finally got it going in first and could shift to second and third gear. Hey, I was feeling great now.

But then Grandpa said, "Stop it again. Put it back into first and make sure you ease the clutch."

I knew now that easing the clutch meant slowly, but the *how slowly* part comes only with experience. Now about three times out of five, I jumped that truck forward and killed the engine. I figured I was getting better, but Grandpa had his handkerchief out and was mopping his face.

And so it went for another long four hours. Finally, I was able to get it out of first three times out of four, and he thought it was logical that I should try some driving with curves, small hills and flat spaces to really let me learn the tricks of shifting. I started sweating and wondered where I was going to go that had little chance of killing some innocent bystander. He said that we would go "around the circle" and Blue Stem Lake where practically no one was, except the occasional cow.

Grandpa drove us all out to Blue Stem and moved over so I could start my practicing again. It was a miracle. I started it out of first the first time, moved into second and then third without sign of a jump, sputter or croak of the engine. And she rolled fine until we came to the low water bridge that is half way around the circle.

That bridge was steep-sided cement with a perfectly flat bottom, with another steep cement side going up. I thought, why not just shift to second, give her a little gas, and I could scoot up that other side of the bridge without shifting? My brain had obviously stopped working, as I did not take into account the steep side going down, the perfectly flat bottom and then the steep side up. I did not share my plan with anyone because, of course, I had it all in hand.

I started down that steep down slope at twenty miles per hour in second gear, and both Grandpa and my dad were screaming at me to slow down, but I kept going, because I knew my plan would work and make them proud.

I hit the flat bottom of that low water bridge on the front tires and when the back tires came down, I was already giving it more gas to shimmy up the other side. Now this is the sticky part—I forgot my brother was in the back of the pickup, and when I bounced those back tires, I bounced him out of the truck slicker than a whistle, and he landed on the shallow water on his butt.

Grandpa reached over, switched off the engine, threw the emergency brake on, and everyone piled out to see if my brother was still kicking.

Oh, he was kicking okay. He came up to me and starting kicking the crap out of me as hard as he could, screaming I had tried to drown him in that shallow water—and what about his butt? He was all bruised and banged up. I told him I was sorry for his butt. I realized the extent of my transgressions and even offered to kiss it to make it better, to which I got the raspberries from my brother. Both Grandpa and Dad were hopping mad as I explained my great plan to them.

Well, after a thoroughly disagreeable discussion with Dad, I started her up again and did it the right way in first on the down slope, the flat slope, and the upward slope. That damn truck did not dare croak on me on that upward slope—I was too pooped and humiliated.

I continued to bounce around the circle, going over cattle guards, missing two cows, hitting one small tree (it was in the road) and finally got it back home.

My grandpa, dad and brother looked like death, and I am sure I did not look much better.

Grandma was there waiting on the front porch for us popping green beans, and she knew the tutoring had been a struggle, especially when she saw my brother limp up the walk to the porch door. Grandpa filled her in on my shifting, and she thought it was a "good start." and tomorrow was another day. After all, she said to Grandpa, "It will teach you patience." Grandpa gave her a glare that would have turned me to stone, but she just smiled and said dinner would be ready in about thirty minutes.

To make a long story short, after two days, I finally got the hang of shifting out of first and reverse and even learned I could skip second gear if I was on a straight and narrow road. I think my wise-ass plans had gone by way of the low water bridge, and my brother looked a little dented for several days. I was sorry I bounced him out of the back of the truck, but when I tried to tell him he bounced real well and he should be proud—that did not work either. He never let me forget I had nearly killed him on the circle, and he never rode with me in the pickup again. I guess he was not as dumb as I thought, even if he was three years younger than me.

In two years it came time for my brother to take a turn at learning the clutching of the old '56, and this time I was in the back of the truck. But I was smart. I roped myself in by tying onto the wheel well and only felt cut in half, not bounced out, when he hit the low water bridge. I looked up through the small back window of the truck. He was looking back at me just smiling. Smug little runt.

My next lesson was running the tractor; I guess we would see who would hold the plow the straightest. But life has little curves in it. I did learn the tractor, but my brother never did. He decided that the '56 would be his truck to drive on the harvest, and I could be on the tractor pulling the wagon. Little poop, he knew where most of the dust and bugs were. I guess he one-upped me on this one, but we sure had some good memories to look back on in our later years. After all, we both lived through it!

To his dying day he still told the story of my dumping him while he limped pathetically around the room. I guess the moral of the story is that younger brothers never forget, because he sure got mileage out of that story, not to mention a few laughs. I am really happy we both survived childhood.

THE CHALLENGE OF MILKING
A GOAT NAMED BILLY
U GA SO TSA NE DV

Grandma, for a while, kept a small band of goats for their milk and cheese. It was often left to me to milk them. Milking a goat is not anything like milking a cow, which I had mastered at a young age. I have really strong hands and learned the motion of squeezing the fingers downward while pulling down on the teat. However, cows just stand there. Goats are not fun creatures.

The first time I ever tried to milk a goat, I found out they have to stand on a small wooden platform so the milker's back does not crack in half before the goat herd is all milked. I also found out that you have to put the right hind foot under your left arm while milking, or they will kick the bucket over.

The first time the bucket was kicked over on me was by Billy the Goat—no you read it right. Grandma named the goats, and this one was Billy. I told her Billy was a boy's name, but she said, "Says who?" and I said, "Yes, Grandma," and went to work.

I often wonder if she had me do this one first because, later, I found out she was the "baddest" one in the whole bunch. On the first milking I was unaware of the foot-holding process, and Billy was half-way milked. Darned if that little devil did not look back at me with her little slit eyes and go "Ne ne ne ne ne ne ne ne ne ne ne ne," and I could swear that a corner of her mouth went up before she hauled off and whapped that bucket off the platform. The milk went all over me, of course. I still believe that this is the equivalent of the universal sign language of "flipping the finger" for goats—at least for Billy.

I started again with old Billy, the girl goat, and pulled the right back leg under my left arm and placed the bucket, again, under the teats. I started out, and with all of her wiggling, it was hard to get a rhythm started—but I persevered and was soon in the swing of things milking old Billy, wiggling and bucking throughout the whole process.

Sure enough, about half way through the whole procedure, she turned and looked back at me and gave me that same dirty look. But this time I was ready and moved the bucket and took a good grip on the right back leg. When old Billy reared back to jump toward the bucket, all she got was air and a dirty look from me. After eyeing each other for a while, I commenced milking and got through the course of action with a lot of sweat and my left arm feeling like it was being torn off.

I moved the bucket down on the floor and started to lead Billy down the ramp to the pen and damned if she did not jump around and kick that bucket and spill the milk.

I don't believe in cruelty to animals, but I was sure thinking that old Billy should be better in a stew about that time. As I counted to ten, I decided to ask Grandma's advice and let Billy go to the pen. Better this than me committing goat murder.

I finished off the other seven goats in about an hour flat. They liked getting milked to relieve that pressure of fullness. They were smart. They must be a different type of goat, I was thinking, or Billy was dropped on her head as a baby or her name had screwed her up mentally, like a boy named Sue.

I asked Grandma's advice, and she told me that Billy had the same bag of tricks. She would: 1) always kick the bucket of milk if she could get to it, 2) she was a real humdinger when it came to milking, and 3) she was contrary and downright pigheaded sometimes. I asked her why she kept that goat, and she said she liked a challenge. I told her I did not like the challenge, but she looked at me and said, "Life is made up of challenges. You best get used to it, Granddaughter." She had me.

Next day, I set out to do the milking, and did the other seven goats first, letting old Billy simmer in the pen so to speak. I came prepared. I had a halter that I put on Billy's head and hooked that to the rail on top of the platform. I also had a high table to place the bucket of milk, so she could not turn and kick it when done, and I had a thicker sleeve on, so her bucking right leg would be easier to hold. Old Billy did not take too well to that halter, and she did her best to chew it off. But I had taken the precaution of smearing it with pepper, so it did not taste so good. I did myself in this time. It seems old Billy was allergic to pepper and went through a real seizure of sneezing and actually bounced off the stand on one good sneeze.

Billy had to be milked that day, or she would be in pain from all of the milk, so I waited until she stopped sneezing and blowing snot all over and up on the platform. Then we went at it again.

This time, she did not try to eat the halter, she tried to eat me. As I was putting the bucket under her, she swung back her head as far as it would go and got a mouthful of my hair in her mouth. When I started to rise up, Billy clamped on that hair just as hard as she could. She had me bent double. We fought it out for a while, her pulling, me pulling, and I decided enough was enough. Who was smarter, the goat or me? I could reach her head, so I grabbed her ear and put my finger in her ear and started rubbing the short hair in her ears. That got her attention. She did not like anyone in her ears. She let go, I let go, and we both just eyeballed each other again.

This next try, I tightened up her halter where she could not reach me, put the bucket under her, grabbed her right back leg, and away we went again. She was either tired or had given up, because I got through this milking without a hitch. I put the bucket up on the table and untied her halter, and off she went into the pen with the others. All the way back to the pen, though, she had her beady eyes on me, just looking for the chance to cause mischief.

That summer went okay, but Billy was always on the watch to cause trouble. She and I had the challenge each day of who would win—her or me. I admit that there were two occasions where she got me, but most of the summer went like clockwork.

Eventually, it came to be the last day of the summer, and my last milking. I led old Billy up to the platform and she behaved herself just like a lady. I guess after a whole summer, she had decided that we were on equal footing in the mischief area. Anyway, that milking was my last of old Billy, as Grandma had switched to Nubian goats the next summer, who were even meaner, but that is another story.

MY FIRST ROUNDUP

My first roundup was when I was twelve, on a seventeen-year-old horse named Lucky. He had been a working cow horse all of his life before being put out to pasture by his owner Bill, a friend of Grandma's. He was a big horse, seventeen hands, and still proud and fine looking for his age. It was decided that I could help round up the small herd of cows Grandma's friend had, with me riding Lucky.

I had been around horses all of my life, so I saddled and bridled him with no problem. After checking him out, to be sure the girth was tight and that the legs and hoofs looked okay, I mounted and off we went.

The herd that Bill and I were moving was out in the grazing land near Blue Stem Lake. It was isolated and very rocky and had many trees. Bill told me to look in the ravine for calves that may have been separated from their mothers during the thunderstorm the night before, so Lucky and I trotted off in that direction.

I know some things about riding, like leaning backward in the saddle when a horse goes downhill, when to give the horse its head, and when to say "whoa!" One thing never covered in any book I had read was Lucky's reaction to the calves.

There were about ten in the ravine, and as we slipped and scooted down the hillside, Lucky got spooked at something nearby or the calves—I am not sure what. Anyway, he started stepping to the side, twitching, and acting very nervous. I considered this not a good sign for a fairly inexperienced cow herder. I looked around and did not hear or see anything that would cause his alarm, nor his continuing alarm. Bill was out of sight, and I just had to wing it.

We got to the bottom of the ravine with me still in the saddle, which I thought was a plus, and Lucky continued to act like a colt on his first outing. It was then that I noticed that all of the calves were gathered together at one end of the ravine, and we were at the other.

Then I heard it, a rattling sound coming from the left of us. I was sure afraid to look over. On that side of the ravine, I saw a round ball of rattle snakes just coming out from hibernation. It looked to be over a hundred of them from where I sat, but of course, my adrenalin was pumping pretty hard at that time. Some of them were as round as my waist and longer than Lucky. Some of them were tiny, no bigger than a large night crawler.

When in doubt, trust in the horse, because he had tons more experience in this stuff than me, so I gave him his head and said, "Go for it!" It wasn't a nanosecond later that saw me on top of Lucky, hanging on for dear life, as he scrambled back up the slick hillside, through rocks, brush, trees, and numerous puddles of water. I gave up all pretense of trying to look good riding. I just hung on for dear life, because if I fell off, I would roll back down the hillside right into the snakes. Did I mention that I have a phobia of snakes?

I shut my eyes, and after Lucky stopped, on what felt to be level ground, I opened them and saw we were back at the top of the hill. Lucky was lathered from the effort, and I was just happy to be alive and shouted, "Thank you, Jesus!"

About that time Bill came along. I explained that there were about ten calves down in the ravine plus about a hundred snakes. He peeked over the side and said the only way to get the calves was to start a fire in the middle of the ravine, and cut the snakes off "at the pass." This would allow Bill to rope each calf and pull it up the hill.

So it went, Bill lit a fire, rolled it down the ravine, and cut the snakes off (plus blistering a few in the process). Bill roped a calf, gave me the rope, I tied it to my saddle, and Lucky and I pulled up the calf, with it bawling and resisting every step. Once up top, I took the rope off, and returned it to Bill to give me another rope with a unhappy little one on the other end. It took us, working together, about two hours to get all of the calves up the ravine, and I don't think I once did not check to see if there were any snakes wiggling around near me.

The rest of the roundup took little time as the cows were on flat ground, and it was just getting used to cutting them off from wandering and keeping them headed in the direction of the corral.

About three hours later, Bill and I had the cows and calves all in the corral and ready for pick up by the trucks later in that day. Lucky looked pooped, but had done me proud, and Bill said he would not have missed the day for anything, as my eyes were as big as saucers when I told him about the snakes. Boy, he thought it was it funny. I told him I was glad I could keep him in stitches, as it sure scared me. Well, that was the end of my cowherding days. I started at the age of twelve and ended at the age of twelve—never to ride the range again. Amen for that.

RECLAIMING GRANDMA'S CHICKEN EGGS
JU WE TSI

Grandma kept a few chickens in the old barn that was in back of the house. My brother Mike and I hated that barn. It was falling down, dark, dirt-floored, and the old tractor took up most of the space inside. On the right hand side of the barn, the chickens had their nests, half way up the wall of the barn. You had to be thin to slide sideways down the side of the barn to get to the chicken nests. Sticking your hand under a chicken in the dark, in old straw, is not always pleasant. It took a lot of spunk. Grandma did not have a flashlight, so my brother and I were pretty much going by Braille.

Every summer holiday, one of our major chores was to get the eggs from the chickens so that Grandma could put some in the fridge and sell some to people who liked fresh eggs. She usually had about three dozen eggs in a week, so that was a goodly amount of eggs from just a few chickens.

The first summer day when we arrived in Pawhuska, Mike and I went to the barn, not actually excited about it, but willing to brave the dark and spider-ridden place for the eggs. It was usually I who went first and did the first nest, he did the second, I did the third, and so on until we got to the tenth nest. We figured that we had a half-and-half chance of getting stung, bitten, or somehow mangled by some unknown entity by sharing the chore half-and-half. Keep in mind we had lively imaginations at the age of thirteen and ten.

The first day was a good one, no bites, but about a dozen eggs. Grandma was pleased. We had a few other things to do, but mostly we ran around the place and explored Bird Creek and saw how dirty we could get playing in the mud and water. Those were the days, catching frogs, wading in the stream, lying under the large trees, looking at clouds and identifying what they looked like, catching tadpoles, using sticks to flip up stones to see what critter was under it, and always ready to run.

We finally convinced Grandma to build a small chicken house outside of the barn after she collected eggs and ran into a black snake. (I really think she convinced herself.) However, I was profoundly thankful that it was not me that had touched that snake. Otherwise, I would not be writing this now, because I would have had a heart attack and be dust.

That summer passed, and soon it was the next summer and Mike and I were ready to go collect the eggs from the new chicken house. We got over there, only stopping to look at the new well, collecting bug shells off the trees, and of course, Mike always collected "cool" looking sticks along the way. He liked to play "camp fire" in the evening with Grandma's supervision. Eventually, we got to the house and saw that the door was open— this was not the way it was supposed to be. Looking in, we both shouted at the same time "Snake!" and jumped on top of the chicken house. Looking through the sides of the wire house, we could see it was a black snake, about three yards long and as thick as a steel fence pole, eating the eggs. Needless to say, the chickens had vacated.

Not that we were bored or anything, but it seemed like a good idea to try to get the eggs back. I am pretty sure that this was Mike's idea, because I was the oldest and would never have thought up such a thing. However, we both ran over to the large trees and found two long branches with a little "Y" shape on the end and jumped back up on the chicken house. We waited and the snake eventually came out, full of eggs, which were easily seen inside of him by little bumps. Mike took the first try, and held the snake's head down, while I maneuvered over and started using my stick to roll the eggs back out through the snake's mouth. We both thought it would not work, but what the hell, it was something new and fun to try.

That snake twisted and rolled, but Mike had it pinned as I poked my stick along its body and rolled an egg to its mouth. Sure enough, Mike moved his stick back, and one popped out, whole and uncracked! Well, this was getting more interesting. Mike wanted a try, so I took the head of the snake, and Mike tried his skill in rolling out the next egg. It worked like a charm, and we laughed and giggled like madmen on top of that little chicken house. We eventually got nine eggs back from that snake, and when the last egg popped, we let the snake go, and it took off across the field like it was being chased by the hounds of hell.

Of course, it took a little longer to collect the eggs this way, but we thought it was worth it, since we had fun and got all the eggs back. We proudly collected all of the eggs and took them back to Grandma. She looked at the outside of the eggs, and asked what was wrong with them, as the shiny protective part was missing from the shells. Mike and I very proudly told her the story of getting the eggs back, and she had a cow. One, we had been messing with a live snake, and two, we could have fallen off the chicken house and been killed. Funny, we never thought of that.

She took the eggs, after telling us a thing or two, and said if that snake turned up again, come and get her and she would get her walking stick and would "beat it in the head and get rid of it."

Each day we went for the eggs, we took our forked sticks along, and each day it was just chickens that were in the house. Sadly, the snake never showed up again. So much for that fun, but we soon found more to do around the farm, and the snake event was forgotten until today as I see my brother and I again, happy and young, on top of the chicken house.

MRS. TANNEYHILL

When I was very small, about five or six years old, my brother, Mike, and I would visit Grandma's closest neighbor, an older woman named Mrs. Tanneyhill. She lived at the end of the long gravel driveway that led up to Grandma's house. It was an old white house, with a chunk of granite for the first step that led into the house. By all accounts, it was pretty run-down, even to us, but it always held warmth and good conversation.

It seems that Mrs. Tanneyhill was a widow and out of her thirteen children, born in that house, only two survived. She talked about the flu, malaria, TB and "fevers" that would come and her young ones would "go home." When we visited her, she always opened a can of biscuits and baked them for us so we would have something to munch on while we talked. I don't remember much about the inside of the house, only the kitchen.

The kitchen was warmed by a cast iron wood-burning stove that sat right in the middle with a long, black stack that ran out the side of the house. It smelled wonderful, and I remember her one time telling us about her parents that had come through Kansas during hard times. She told us that they had all lived in a sod house for two years in Kansas until her father had died at the age of thirty-two when a horse kicked him in the head. She said that her mother and her siblings, numbering six, moved from place to place while her mother sewed for a living and took other odd jobs to support the family.

Mrs. Tanneyhill always wore wire-rim glasses that looked a little yellow next to her snow white hair, and a white apron that covered the whole front of her dress and tied around her neck and waist. I never saw her without that apron. She had made lace to go around it, and that was where I got my first lesson on tatting and the use of the shuttle and how to do patterns for lace.

Mike and I loved to visit her as she always had good stories to tell and things to show us. One of the visits I remember quite well.

It was nearing the end of summer vacation, and we had just eaten a whole pan of biscuits while chatting with Mrs. Tanneyhill. She reached over and stood on her tip toes to reach on a top shelf in the kitchen and brought down what looked like two hair brushes, but bigger and with porcupine-quill bristles. We asked what they were, and she told us that these were used in cleaning wool, before it was spun on the spinning wheel. She said that a lot of weeds and pieces of things got caught in the wool, and even after washing, it and had to be brushed until it was straight and clean before being spun.

Then she told us about the sheep her mother had kept and how they would spin for hours to make wool thread for selling at the town's general store or for bartering for what they needed. One year she got a pair of shoes for the winter from the store with a summer's worth of spinning. She then showed us a wooden spool that was much bigger than regular thread spools and a spinning wheel. She demonstrated with some wool hank how it was done. She used her feet to turn the wheel, while her nimble fingers would stretch and pull on the wool to make it even and the same size as it twisted and turned onto the spool. She made it look easy, but I don't think it was. She explained that she now did her own wool thread and made sweaters for others for the winter as gifts. I asked her why she did not sell them, as it sure looked like she could use the money. This is the part that I remember the most—she said, "Some things are worth more than money or all the gold in the world: happiness, love and the gift of giving to those who need."

Sometimes Mike and I would pull the bigger weeds and brush that was around her house so she would be able to get out easier; sometimes we just talked.

We had a lot of interesting conversations with her over the years we visited Grandma, and later, when I was an adult, I heard that she had fallen in the winter and died of the cold on her front step one night. It wasn't too much longer before someone tore her house down, and there is no trace now of what was once a place of comfort and teaching for two youngsters.

I later asked what Grandma knew of Mrs. Tanneyhill, and she said that she knew little—only that she was a widow, lived in that same house for as long as she knew, and had two children who came to see her off and on. She said it was her children who had the house torn down, and Grandma bought the land, which was attached to her own land.

Many years after that my brother and I would walk down that gravel driveway and look over at where the house had been and remember the many stories she shared with us. We were lucky to have had the opportunity to have her share so much. She could not have known how much she affected myself and my brother—I know we both held more of a reverence for things we had taken for granted. But maybe she did know —maybe she just did not want her stories to be forgotten.

As I write, her stories live again. She is still alive in my mind, and second by second, I can see her smiling and spinning and taste those biscuits again. I guess she will always be alive to me as long as I live, and visit her again from time to time in my memories. Even though Mrs. Tanneyhill has "gone home," her life's wisdom lives on.

ATTACK GEESE
SA SA

One year Grandma called us and said that she thought she saw someone sneaking around the house, and she had gotten a pair of geese to guard the place. I thought, geese, why geese?

That summer, as usual, I visited Grandma and met her two geese. They were larger than I expected, about up to my throat, and I was four feet tall. They used to run around with their wings outstretched and chase me across the yard. It seemed that they were territorial also.

It then became a challenge how to get out of the house and not have the attack geese pinch me with their beaks and squawk up a storm as they chased me, in a rapid manner, across the yard.

First, I reasoned, they could probably be bribed with food—dogs could! So the next step was, what do geese eat? I did not want to ask Grandma, as I thought she would think me a dummy at my old age of eleven, not knowing what geese ate. I remember feeding ducks old bread at a pond, so I decided to try bread. I took a whole loaf of bread, tore it up into little pieces, and threw it out the front door, being sure that the geese brothers heard me. Out they flew across the yard and started squawking at me behind the screen porch door. I pointed to the bread, and they disdainfully ignored it.

Now I was wondering how I was going to tell Grandma how one of her fresh loafs of bread ended up in the front yard. I was sort of counting on the geese to clean it up. Not to linger on that problem, I started thinking what else could I do to distract them? Reasoning again, I thought they lived in the water, so maybe they liked fish.

Hot dog! Grandma was taking care of some gold fish for the neighbor, so I thought she would not miss two or three. Fishing those little suckers out was fun, I can tell you that. Once accomplished, I put my hand through the screen door, gold fish in sight, and called to the geese. Grandma named every other animal she owned, but she just called the geese "Geese" for names. So, I yelled, "Here geese, here geese." One was just around the corner and flew by and grabbed the fish and pinched my hand in a most vicious manner. Well, they liked fish, but they still disliked me. So I tried it again, "Here geese, here geese" and both turned up in the front yard. I slowly extended my hand and flicked the two remaining gold fish into the grass for them and waited to see what happened. Sure enough, they both liked the fish and they gobbled them down. Then they turned around to me and just stared.

Taking that as a good sign, I sort of eased out the door, down the step, and started walking to the swing in the old oak tree. I got about half way there and they started honking and flapping their wings and running toward me. I was trapped! The steep hill was before me, and the geese were behind me, so I did the only sensible thing. I scrambled up the tree. But I was not quite fast enough. As I was scrambling, one of the geese brother's beaks slid against my leg and caught in my underwear. Now remember, this is before little girls really wore anything but dresses. Geese beaks also have little sharp points on them.

I was embarrassed, mad and stuck. I could not go up without pulling my pants off, or pulling a goose with me, and could not go down without being the object of extensive pecking.

It was a good thing that Grandma looked out the window to see what the ruckus was, because I probably would be in the same dilemma now—I did not want to have a bare butt, and I sure did not want to pull a goose into the tree with me. I could just see it beating me with its big wings and scratching me with the nails on its big webbed feet.

She took stock of what was what pretty quickly and came running with a broom. It did not take her too long to pop the geese on their sides, and as they stared little holes in her, she whopped them again.

The goose that was stuck to my pants did not let go during this rumble, but his brother ran for the hills. Grandma reached up and took that goose hanging from me by the neck and popped his head off me faster than a cork in a bottle. All in one sweeping motion, she had the goose off me and pushed him across the yard with the broom, and all the time she was yelling at the top of her lungs in Cherokee. I caught the words "no good," but thankfully could not make out the rest.

Broom still in hand, she came back over to me and asked if I was okay. I told her the geese were a menace and hated me. She asked me if I had fed them some cracked corn before coming out, and I said, "What is cracked corn?" She looked at me like I was a dummy. She reached into a bucket by the front door and pulled out kernels of corn that had been cracked into smaller pieces. This she threw out into the front yard and asked me to yell "Geese, geese." The geese brothers came running up to the front door and ate that corn. She then told me it was okay to go out, as she had trained them herself to ignore anyone who fed them cracked corn.

I pointed out that she had fed them, but she said I had called them. I was not the one that was going to be telling my grandma that she was full of hooey, so I limply stepped out the front door, while she watched, and attempted to walk across to the swing again. I had the tree lined up just in case, though. Sure enough, those stupid geese completely ignored me. It became a big joke in our family about cracked corn and me. Anytime I was afraid to do anything, someone would yell "Throw some cracked corn" and then die laughing.

I wish I had a good proverb or ending to this, but the geese brothers lived on and guarded her house until old age, and they passed on to goose heaven. What I learned was: Ask and you shall receive—or endure the circumstances. It is much better to ask.

GRANDMA'S NOSE
KA YA SA

One summer my brother and I stayed with my grandparents for two weeks. Grandma ran a bar and grill downtown, the Osage Bar and Grill, and often our days were spent with Grandpa while she ran back and forth to work. I remember one day that we (Grandpa, my brother and I) all thought we could cook some green beans, squash, baked sweet potatoes and fish for dinner. Grandpa was not sure how to go about this, so my brother and I took charge. We were in our early teens, and this was a great new experience—we were doing dinner!

My brother decided that he would light the barbeque, and I decided to help him. The problem was—we had never lit one before. Of course, we had observed our elders doing this, and it looked pretty easy. So we dumped a whole bag of charcoal into the grill, which was a half a steel drum on legs, and we knew we needed to have some lighter fluid or something to get it started. Lo and behold, right there by the grill, under the carport, was a gallon can of gas.

We decided that it probably needed the whole gallon, because there were so many briquettes in the grill. We knew enough to stay back when we threw the match. Otherwise, we might burn our eyelashes off. As it was, we singed our eyebrows off. Before we knew what was happening, there was a giant fireball that leaped up out of that grill. It looked alive, and it commenced to get the grill glowing red hot. It actually melted one of the steel legs so it looked lopsided.

Also, we did not know that waiting is good when charcoaling, to let the coals die down and get consistent heat. After all, we reasoned, there was a lid, and that would squash the flames as the stuff cooked. So I wrapped the potatoes in three layers of deluxe aluminum foil; wrapped the chicken in five layers, with barbeque sauce in it; and put the squash and green beans on the stove to cook. Everything went in fine, and there was plenty of room on the grill. We shut the lid and decided to play on the old swing on the tall tree that swung over the hillside while it cooked. We figured it would take about two hours or so to cook clear through. We were wrong.

Before we knew what was happening, Grandpa came out and said something was burning in the house and what was the black smoke coming out from under the car port where the barbeque grill was? My brother took the grill, and I took the kitchen. Grandma's stove used gas, and I was not used to a real flame when cooking, since my parents had electric. The beans were black and stuck to the bottom of the stewer, and the squash looked like mush from hell. Grandpa said to dump both outside because Grandma could always smell stuff that burned. She hated her house smelling like that. We opened all the windows in the house, sprayed air freshener, and cleaned all of the pans.

Outside, my brother was having his own problem. When he opened the grill, the fire was still licking the lid of the grill, and it had burned off all of the aluminum foil. The only thing left were tiny burned chunks of fish and potatoes. That is what it had to be—we could not recognize anything. We all decided to dump this over the hill and go out for dinner. We would tell Grandma that we forgot to cook. That seemed a great resolution to the problem.

The only problem was Grandma came home early, walked in the door, asked what was burning, why the car port had a black roof, and why the grill was melted on one side nearly to the ground? We all owned up to our misfortune in trying to help her out with cooking, and she said she knew something was on fire, as the fire department had called after seeing the black smoke rising near her house.

In punishment, we had to eat what she thought was the best for us that night: wild onions with eggs, poke salad, whole fish cooked in corn meal and lard, and squaw bread. I confess we mostly ate the fish and bread—but she made sure that we ate some of the rest also "on principal."

It was many years later before either my brother or I ever used a grill again. I still get the shakes if I have to cook on one, because I can still see my grandmother's eyes staring me down, picking the thoughts out of my brain that I had almost burned the house down.

DRAGGING THE GUT WITH GRANDMA

When in Pawhuska, it was always the custom for Grandma and me to "Drag the Gut" which meant riding up and down the main street to see what was going on. We did this as often as possible after any excursion. The main street in Pawhuska is called *Kihekha* and runs from east to west. It is about ten short blocks long. Even though it runs right by the police station, most people go faster than the standard twenty miles an hour.

One Sunday, Grandma and I were coming back from picking chokecherries and had four baskets full in the back seat of the car, along with our red hands and mouths. As it happened, we were stopped at the light by the triangle building (the middle of the block) and a young man pulled up in what would now be called a "muscle car," a '76 Mustang, revving the engine and shouting out the window. Grandma looked calmly over at the young man and asked what he wanted. He said that he could, "Clobber an old woman driving a big car," and did she want to drag? Now, this was before seat belts, and also her car was a new Cadillac with a V-8 engine with overdrive.

If there was one thing that my grandmother could not pass up, it was a challenge. I had a really bad feeling about this as she put her left foot on the brake and commenced to revving her car to match the noise level of his car. I tried reason and told her that the police station was just down the block, and we could go to jail dragging down main street. She smiled sweetly at me and said, "Don't worry, I have enough money to get us out." I broke out in hives.

The light down the block was changing to green, and I knew it was just a matter of time before our light changed to green also. All during this interminable few minutes, both cars were growling and making little jumps forward. Now is a good time to remember that my grandmother was only 4' 2", and she used to sit on the

Tulsa Yellow Pages so she could see out the window to drive the car. More about this later.

Well, the inevitable happened. The light turned green, both cars popped forward, and I looked briefly over at Grandma. She was leaning as far forward as she could get on the wheel and still reach the accelerator pedal. She had that car floored.

Both cars raced for about six blocks before anything happened, and then it happened with such quickness, it was hard to follow. The Mustang, seeing that he was not going to win this race quickly, cut in front of Grandma, and in her reflex to miss the Mustang she hit the brake. Several things were set in motion like a ripple effect: as she swerved the car, she hit the brakes; the chokecherries started flying over the seat and hitting the front windshield making it a sloppy red; I had a grip on the door handle for dear life; her butt slid off her phone book as the car was stopping and she landed in the floorboard; and the car kept going forward as her foot slipped off the brake. I knew then that the Lord was coming to take us home.

They say that you don't remember the last few minutes of your life, and I don't remember things for a few minutes, because the next thing I knew the car was stopped, she was out of the car, and she was chasing that Mustang down the street on foot.

When she hit the floor, she must have clamped her hands down on the brake to stop the car, because, Lord have mercy, we were stopped. That poor youngster did not have a chance. The next light turned red, and instead of going ahead and jumping it, he stopped and my tiny grandmother caught up with him.

She reached in the window, grabbed his ear, and started telling him the positive attitude he should have toward his elders, since she now recognized him as one of the leading citizen's sons. She finally let him go and calmly got back into the car, and we drove home. The next day not only did she get a written apology from his dad, but four baskets of chokecherries were delivered at the front door.

I asked her how she had gotten this done, as she had also been dragging the kid too. She looked at me with those dark eyes and cocked her head to the side and said, "I simply reminded his father, by phone last night, that I had taught him how to treat his horses for the bloating when he had allowed them to overeat on his dad's farm. I thought it was about time that his dad knew how he had learned this cure."

It just goes to show that if you live long enough, you know enough about everyone to get what you want done. In this case, she considered she had won the race by "default" and we canned the chokecherries that day.

THE VOICE OF EQUALITY

Grandma always believed that everyone was equal to everyone else. This always held true, until she decided that someone just could not understand why people should be equal. If that happened she would mumble "too stupid —need to get their beans in a row." This did not happen often, as she always looked for the best in everyone. If she could not find anything worth saving, she would just walk away.

The one time she walked away, was when she tried to help a stranger bandage a deep cut on his leg. He had been cutting grass with a bare blade and had a deep gash on his lower back leg. We were driving by and saw him trying to stem the blood and stopped.

The man took one look at my grandmother's wizened dark face and her bag of medicines and started trying to make up reasons why he needed no help.

Grandmother was patient. She told him she was a healer, and at the very least, she could get the blood to stop so he could go to his physician of choice. He argued some, but he had to sit down because of loss of blood, and Grandma used this time to tie off his wound so it would bleed little. The man was woozy when he sat down, but once she got the bandage on his leg, he popped up (on one leg) and promptly told her that he did not want any "Red Indian medicine" around him. He said he had been told what Indians do to people. She looked him straight in the eyes, after stopping, taking her time, energy, knowledge and bandages, and said, "You had best get over your ignorance, or you will find that you just might miss what the Creator has provided you." The guy just looked at her, after all she was very short and he was over six feet, and contemplated her words.

Grandma said it was time we were off, and as we were leaving the guy mumbled a tight-lipped "Thanks." Grandma said "Welcome" and got in the car.

As we were driving along, she told me that some people are born that hold prejudices against people with different skin colors or different cultures, and they were told to suspect motives. I asked her why anyone would want to teach this to their children. She said that they did not listen to the Creator, but to what others told them—ones that did not listen to the Creator.

I asked her how we could change this, and she said, "We just did. That man will get to the doctor soon and will find out that the wound was deep and that if it had not been bound tightly in a cross-wise manner by bandages, he could have surely gone into shock and possibly died." I asked if she thought this kind act would make a difference in the world? She said no, but little things done for others, little by little, would promote change. She always believed that she should treat others as she wanted to be treated herself.

This was my first brush with prejudice against Native Americans, and I was shocked to think that a stranger would refuse help just because of the color of someone's skin. It was a hard lesson, but buffered by my grandmother's wisdom.

DEATH: A NEW BEGINNING

Death was a thing my grandmother made sure I knew about. From our first days together, she told me of the Creator, the next life, and the way things were when someone died.

She said that people missed those who moved on, but those who passed were in a place that lacked nothing. There was no pain, no sickness, no poverty and everyone was happy. She used the example also in the Bible that the body was just a tent, and when we died, the real essence of our life, moved to the next cycle of life. She said that she felt that nothing was wasted in this cycle of being born, dying and moving on. She had only to look at the seasons and see the vision of the Creator to know this.

She took me to my first funeral, a traditional White funeral. It was not what I expected. There was no joy; there was only sadness and those at the funeral looked at the body as the place the person still was. I asked her about this, and she said that some people thought the body was the closest they could come to their loved one, and so they kept it tended in a fancy box with metal shells.

She said that it did not matter what happened to the body when the spirit was gone, as it had served its purpose and should go back to the earth. I had never thought about death before this, and now I understood that I would die also someday. It was an epiphany.

The next funeral she took me to was a Cherokee funeral. There was a gathering of all of the relatives and friends, and traditional dancing was often included in the ceremony. There was ritual, and people were sad they could no longer talk to the person, but there was not such grief. The loved one had gone to the next step in life—food was given for the journey, and the sacred fire was lit to help show them the way. This ceremony often took two or three days. But it was more than a ceremony; it was a celebration of that person's life. Many who attended told stories of happy memories.

Many sacred herbs and plants were used in these ceremonies, and often it was Grandma who provided them.

When my grandmother died, I was so sad at first that I failed
to remember her words, that she was passing to a better place. I
remember stroking the bison-bone beads and thinking of all the
things she had told me of the Nation. I found myself wondering if
these things would all survive when the elders died.

One of the main reasons I wanted to write these stories was I
am the last female in the Dawes line. I have no daughter to teach
the skills of healing and of the Nation. So I am doing the next best
thing. I am leaving specific memories for my family and those who
seek knowledge about the Cherokee. I hope the wisdom of my
grandmother shines through the pages and that she looks upon
this work as one from my heart.

I am sure she would look at this writing and say, "You left out
so many of the traditional stories. You should have done the herb
descriptions more carefully." It is okay, Grandma. You have a
granddaughter who does not have your skill, but who uses her
heart to write this.

PAMELA DAWES TAMBORNINO

Pamela Dawes Tambornino (Cherokee, Wolf Clan) teaches at Haskell Indian Nations University in Lawrence, KS. She received her Bachelor of Arts degree in English, Magna Cum Laude, at Washburn University and a Master of Library Science degree at Emporia State University. She is completing a Master of Arts in English at Emporia State University. She won the Federal Librarian of the Year from the Library of Congress in 2001 while working at Haskell, and the Ted Fleming Teaching Award from Washburn University for teaching excellence. She has published in *Tribal College Journal*, the *Chicken Soup for the Soul* series, and *Yellow Medicine Review*.

MAMMOTH PUBLICATIONS BOOKS

Barnes, Barry — *We Sleep In a Burning House: Poems* $10

Day, Robert — *We Should Have Come by Water: Poems* $10

Glancy, Diane — *Stories of the Driven World: Poems* $14

Stories of the Driven World, Hardback $24

Low, Denise & Tom Weso — *Langston Hughes in Lawrence,* $15 paper, $24 hardback

Low, Denise, ed. — *To the Stars: Kansas Poets Project* $12

Low, Denise — *New & Selected Poems* (rpt., 2nd ed.) $15

Meyers, Lana — *Biography of May Williams Ward,* $15

Milk, Theresa — *Haskell Institute: 19th Century Stories* $20

Mirriam-Goldberg, Caryn — *Landed: Poems* $12

Landed: Poems & CD, Kelley Hunt $20

Schultz, Elizabeth — *White-Skin Deer: Hoopa Stories* $10

Tambornino, Pamela — *Maggie's Story: Cherokee Teachings* $14

Two-Rivers, E. Donald — *Fat Cats, Powwows, & Other Indian Tales:* $12

Order Online:

www.mammothpublications.com (Pay Pal)
mammothpubs@hotmail.com

Mail Order, add $3. Kansas residents add 6.3%.

Mammoth Publications
1916 Stratford Rd. Lawrence, KS 66044